Making All Things Well

Isobel de Gruchy is a South African by birth and upbringing. She is married to an ordained minister who is also a theologian, and has three children. She has lived through the struggle against and demise of Apartheid, and more recently, the tragic death of her eldest son, also a theologian.

Her Christian faith has been the guiding force in her life, and she has been involved in church life through such things as writing Sunday School curricula, leading Bible Study groups and running volunteer organizations. Now retired and living on Volmoed, a Christian Retreat and Conference Centre in Hermanus in South Africa's Western Cape, she pursues her interest in art and poetry; exhibiting her art, learning how to 'write' icons, self-publishing collections of poetry and a book of meditations. Julian of Norwich has for years been a source of great insight and assurance in her faith, resulting in this collection of poems and meditations.

Making All Things Well

Finding spiritual strength with
Julian of Norwich

Isobel de Gruchy

CANTERBURY
PRESS

Norwich

© Isobel de Gruchy 2012

First published in 2012 by the Canterbury Press Norwich
Editorial office
3rd Floor, Invicta House,
108–114 Golden Lane,
London EC1Y 0TG

Canterbury Press is an imprint of Hymns Ancient & Modern Ltd
(a registered charity)
13A Hellesdon Park Road, Norwich,
Norfolk, NR6 5DR, UK

www.canterburypress.co.uk

Scripture quotations taken from the New Revised Standard Version of the Bible, Anglicized Edition, copyright © 1989, 1995, by
the Division of Christian Education of the National Council of
the Churches of Christ in the USA. Used by permission. All rights
reserved.

British Library Cataloguing in Publication data

A catalogue record for this book is available
from the British Library

978 1 84825 240 0

Originated by the Manila Typesetting Company
Printed and bound by CPI Group
(UK) Ltd, Croydon, CR0 4YY

Contents

Contents

To Judy and Sadie,
my fellow 'Hazelnutters',
gracious and familiar friends,
in well and in woe.

Foreword

Ours is a highly competitive culture. The qualities that are praised are the masculine ones and those who are admired, perhaps envied, are the hugely successful men and women who exhibit these qualities: the ones who have aggressively fought their way to the top, pushing aside any opposition in their path; who keep their eye on the goal and do not allow sentiment to interfere. In the Church, we too have been infected. Our God was for many centuries described almost exclusively in masculine terms – Father, King, Lord; the Bible, hymns and liturgies have spoken of the Saviour of 'mankind', and call 'men' to redemption. We have become more and more aware that this has led to a distortion that impoverished us grievously.

Julian of Norwich, the fourteenth-century English mystic, through her *Revelations of Divine Love*, is one who has helped to provide a corrective to restore the balance. For her, quite boldly and amazingly, Jesus is our 'Mother' carrying us in his womb to term, looking on us with mercy, with compassion, with pity but never with blame. Julian is adamant that she never saw any wrath in God and sin was 'no thing'. She has helped recall us to the profound truths about God who is not aggressively masculine, but also feminine in being gentle, compassionate and who will ensure that all manner of things shall be well.

Many profound truths can be communicated only through poetry. Isobel de Gruchy is an accomplished poet and artist. The unpublished anthology of poems that I have, whose contents are all included in this book, is now for me a treasured companion to Lady Julian's *Revelations*. I am particularly indebted to her for helping me to understand the story of the Lord and his Servant. I was more than just a little puzzled by that story. After reading Isobel's poem I understood the illustration better. As an oblate of the Order of Julian of Norwich, I am obliged to read portions daily of the *Revelations of Divine Love*. Isobel's poems, meditations and prayers, all based on the *Revelations*, take us to the heart of Julian's profound spirituality. The forty sections make the book a very useful resource for Lent, but it is more than a book for one season of the Christian Year. I therefore cannot commend it highly enough.

Desmond Tutu
Archbishop Emeritus of Cape Town

Introduction

My encounter with Julian of Norwich

In 1983 I obtained a copy of Julian of Norwich's classic book entitled *Showings*, translated by Edmund Colledge and James Walsh. I did not make much headway with it, so I set it aside. A few years later I acquired a copy of Father John-Julian's translation, published as *A Lesson of Love*. This was easier to follow, and I became absorbed in what this remarkable woman had to say. At the time I was part of a small group of women, all white, middle-aged and South African, who met weekly for prayer and meditation. We were looking for a focus for our meetings and decided to read and discuss *A Lesson of Love*. South Africa was a land in turmoil at the time and it was not easy to buy copies for everyone so I photocopied the text. We felt no compunction in writing all over our copied versions, which we did as, week by week, we read a portion at home and discussed it when we met. To begin with we did not use any other resource, apart from the Bible, in our discussions. Julian spoke to each of us. She took us to the heights of spirituality but was also very down to earth. We did not understand everything but found what she said very special and pertinent to our lives during the upheavals in our country, the 'evil' that surrounded us. In this way we worked our way to the end of the book. By now we had managed to buy a few other books on Julian to find out more about her.

I subsequently read the Colledge and Walsh translation, and through the years that followed kept returning to Julian's writings in that version. On the surface it is strange that she can speak so meaningfully to our age, in which appreciation of her writings continues to grow. Thomas Merton ranked Julian as one of the greatest English theologians, and Archbishop Rowan Williams also holds her in high regard.

Who was Julian?

Many people have said to me, 'Oh yes, I've heard of Julian of Norwich, but who exactly was she?' On learning that she was a fourteenth-century mystic, contemplative and anchoress, they look puzzled or roll their eyes. We know very little about her, not even her real name. It has long been thought that she took her name from the Church of St Julian in Norwich where she lived. She is also affectionately known as Lady or Dame Julian or Juliana. She was born in about 1342 and died, we can tell (from legacies left to her in wills), well on into the fifteenth century at a considerable age. We do know that she was thirty years old when, on 8 May 1373, she suffered from an illness that almost resulted in her death. It was during this time that she received the series of sixteen 'revelations', or 'showings' as she more often called them, from God. When she recovered she became an anchoress who, for the rest of her life, lived in a cell attached to the Church of St Julian in Norwich. She almost certainly had some form of education, although she claims to be 'unlettered'. Perhaps by that she simply meant she had little or no knowledge of Latin.

Why did she write?

Julian wrote down her visions and teachings for her 'fellow Christians' because she saw that this is what God intended by giving her the revelations. She wrote particularly for contemplatives, and spoke about 'contemplation' being the greatest honour a soul can pay to God. She first recorded her visions in a short version, presumably not too long after they occurred. And for the next twenty years she meditated or contemplated on what God and Jesus, her saviour, had revealed to her. With an insight that came from a thorough knowledge of Scripture as well as the writings of other Christian mystics, she then recounted in a longer version how she had wrestled with the questions that her visions invoked in her. However, her writings remained largely unknown until they were translated from the Middle English in which Julian wrote and thus came to life for an increasing number of Christians during the second half of the last century. This is the first book known to be written by a woman in English, and is now acknowledged all over the world as one of the great classics of spiritual literature.

In her revelations or showings we meet a woman who seems in many ways to be a contemporary of ours – a person full of good sense and warmth, whose religious experience is expressed in vivid imagery and gentle humanity. She tells us what she herself was shown by God regarding human nature and how we can grow into unity with God, as well as about the nature of God the blessed Trinity, and above all of his unending love for us. On the surface her theology seems simple, but it is highly complex and carefully woven into an integrated whole. While she is medieval in outlook she often breaks with contemporary thought and introduces a new way of seeing the faith. Julian may seem to be repetitive in her writings, but each time she is revealing more meaning and connecting different aspects to move the reader to a different level. It is as though we were climbing a conical mountain on a spiral walk, seeing the same views again and again, but from a higher vantage point. We could call her writings a 'spiral of love', in stark contrast to the 'spiral of violence' we know so well.

The contemporary reader will undoubtedly find some of Julian's theological language somewhat strange or problematic. She speaks vividly about the 'blood of Jesus', calls Jesus 'our Mother', and uses terms like 'essence' and 'substance' that no longer have the precise meaning they had in the theology of her time. She was immersed in the Bible and in Christian tradition and drew deeply from these resources in giving expression to her faith. We need to enter her world in our imaginations and translate her 'lessons of love' into learnings that apply to ours. So let us do this together; and one of the ways we can do this is through poetry.

Julian's writings expressed in poetry

In September 2009, I started to reread Julian's writings using the Colledge and Walsh translation. I felt strongly that I had to express what I was reading and what Julian was saying to me personally. I started by summarizing her writings and then, while trying to absorb them further, went deeper – from my mind, as it were, into my heart. I started to express what I was feeling in poetry. Poetry seeks to distil truth and express it in a way that enables one to catch a vision of new insights and possibilities. I only realized later that, when I had started to do this, it was twenty years since I had first encountered this woman who was now so dear to me. It had taken me that long to absorb what she had to say, in the same way that it took her twenty years to write down what she finally understood about her visions.

I was still busy with this when, on 21 February 2010, our eldest son, Steve – a husband, father and also a theologian, with so much still to give – died tragically. Julian's writings were and continue to be a tremendous consolation during a time of severe testing of my faith. I continued to write the poems till June 2010. When I showed them to friends they encouraged me to make them available to a wider readership. It was suggested that in order to make them more accessible I should embed them in meditations, which I have happily done. Very recently I came across Fr John-Julian's new book, *The Complete Julian of Norwich*, which I have found helpful in the final stages of preparing my book.

Thanks

One of the members of our original group, affectionately known as the 'Hazelnutters', Judy Cooke, read the poems and the more recent meditations and has helped me immensely with her comments. I am deeply grateful to her for this and also for her encouragement. I also appreciate the support over many years that Sadie Stegmann has given. I thank Helen Hacksley who went over my manuscript and enabled me to improve its language and presentation. My appreciation also goes to the Volmoed community where we live – they are always there for me. I am encouraged by my daughter Jeanelle at all times, for which I thank her. To John, my husband, I owe my poetry writing, my understanding of theology, my pursuing the publishing of my writing and my ability to take the next step when I felt discouraged – love indeed.

I do pray that you, the reader, whether you know Julian as a homely and familiar friend or whether you are meeting her for the first time, may find much in this book that will enrich and inspire you in your journey of faith.

Isobel de Gruchy

Volmoed
May 2012

Acknowledgements

I have quoted excerpts from *Julian of Norwich: Showings – translated from the critical text with an introduction*, translated by Edmund Colledge OSA and James Walsh SJ, in The Classics of Western Spirituality series, Copyright © 1978 by Paulist Press. Used by permission of Paulist Press, www.paulistpress.com. These are acknowledged in the text by (Colledge & Walsh, Chapter no., page no.).

All other quotes from Julian's book are in my own words. I acknowledge the use I have made of Edmund Colledge and James Walsh, as well as the translations of Fr John-Julian. I have kept Julian's use of the male gender for God, but not for people. These are followed only by the chapter number.

The poems are all original, written by myself.

The icon of Julian of Norwich is an original icon painted by myself.

Note on Translation and Word Usage

Julian frequently uses a number of words that are no longer common these days, or whose meaning has changed in the intervening centuries. These often have special significance and so have been retained by some translators. They give her writings their unique flavour. Where I have used more modern words, the older word follows in brackets. Here are some examples of word choices:

God gave Julian sixteen 'showings'. She prefers this word to 'revelations'.

God is 'courteous', which meant 'courtly' or formal and is usually translated as gracious, but at the same time he is 'homely', which meant 'home-like' or informal, translated now as familiar or intimate.

One of Julian's attributes for God or Jesus is 'sweet', which today often comes across as meaning saccharine or cloyingly sweet. In Julian's day it meant 'beloved', a sense we still find today in the word 'sweetheart', and so I have retained it.

Julian refers to the Devil in places as the Fiend. This is translated as 'fiend' by Edmund Colledge and James Walsh, translators of *Showings*, but as 'Fiend' by Fr John-Julian in *A Lesson of Love*. I have used Fiend and Devil in the upper case unless in a quote.

Meditation 1

Wishes and Sickness

As a deer longs for flowing streams, so my soul longs for you, O God.
My soul thirsts for God, for the living God.
When shall I come and behold the face of God?

Psalm 42.1–2

We each come to our Christian faith in different ways. For some of us there is a definite moment to remember, for others there never was a time when we were not Christian. For a young woman living in or around Norwich, in East Anglia, in the fourteenth century, both of these applied. She tells us of a remarkable and very memorable series of what she called 'showings' (or revelations) that she had. But for some time before that she had been a devout believer. For she also tells us that she had long 'desired three graces by the gift of God' (Chapter 2). We all have some things we desire or wish for in our Christian lives. If you had to name three wishes, what would they be? Julian's three were these:

My wish was for God to give me three graces: the first was to experience, as though I were present, Christ's Passion; the second was a bodily sickness; and the third was three wounds. I already felt deeply about Christ's Passion but I longed for more. I wanted, by God's grace, to feel as though I were actually there with Mary Magdalene and Jesus' other friends – to see with my own eyes what he suffered for me. I wanted to suffer with him as others who loved him had done.

Chapter 2

The second grace she asked for strikes us today as very strange. She desired a 'bodily sickness', something just short of actual death. Being aware that even then this was unusual, she added that the first two graces should fall within God's will for her.

On the eighth day of May in 1373, God granted Julian's second 'wish' and along with it the first. She tells us she was thirty and a half years old when she fell seriously ill. When it seemed as though death was near, her curate was sent for; he gave her the Last Rites and held a crucifix in front of her. As she felt death closing in she remembered her wish for the second wound – that Christ's pains would be her pains – to lead her nearer to God. She then saw Christ on the cross as he hung in agony:

> Suddenly I saw the red blood streaming down, freely and copiously, from under the crown of thorns, a living stream, just as it had done when the crown was first pushed onto his blessed head. It came to me, truly and powerfully, that he, who is both God and a man, and who suffered for me, was now showing this to me without any intermediary.
>
> *Chapter 4*

In this way the first of her 'showings' (visions or revelations) began. We will examine these and their meanings in the meditations that follow.

What of the third grace she desired? Again it was unusual then as it is now. It was for three wounds, and these she knew were according to God's will.

> Julian did not ask for three wishes –
> the kind of wishes we might ask for –
> she prayed instead for three wounds,
> not shying away from the pain that these would cause.

'I pray first of all for true contrition:
to see my own shortcomings,
how I enthrone my ego,
and squander my gifts.

Next I pray for loving compassion:
for the gift of a deep love for others,
to feel their pain and the pain of the world,
that it might move me into loving action,
even though I feel I can do so little.

I ask for the wound of longing
with my will for God –
O, the will –
that power which lies deep within,
and short-circuits my best intentions,
that forms a hard shell around my self,
and resists giving over to God –
how I long for my will to conform to God's will for me.'

Based on Chapter 2

Can we say that we are in wholehearted agreement with Julian in this regard? Are any of the things you most long for the same as Julian's? Do you in fact know what it is that you long for the most? We often hide our deepest longings from others and even from ourselves.

A Prayer

Lord, help me to see what it is that I long for most.
Lead me to contrition and compassion.
May my will be conformed to your will.
Then grant me my heart's desire. Amen.

Meditation 2

The Hazelnut and Other Showings

Let the same mind be in you that was in Christ Jesus, who, though he was in the form of God, did not regard equality with God as something to be exploited, but emptied himself, taking the form of a slave, being born in human likeness. And being found in human form, he humbled himself and became obedient to the point of death – even death on a cross.

Philippians 2.5–8

Does God, who is the creator of all, the Lord of lords and King of kings, seem at times too exalted, remote and powerful to be concerned with such insignificant, fallible creatures as ourselves? And what about the whole idea and expression of God as Trinity? Is it so difficult to imagine that you, like me, largely ignore the concept? Right at the beginning of her showings God appears to Julian as triune: 'And in the same revelation, suddenly the Trinity filled my heart full of the greatest joy . . . For the Trinity is God, God is the Trinity' (Colledge & Walsh, Chapter 4, page 181).

In my mind's eye,
when I try to see God,
how hard it is to shut out the old man on his throne;
hard to see God as Mother as well as Father.
Jesus the man I can see,
and the Spirit as amorphous power and presence,
but each stands alone, a separate reality.

For Julian God is the Trinity
and the Trinity is God.
She could see the Trinity as our maker,
our protector and everlasting lover.
The Trinity is our endless joy and our bliss.
When Jesus appeared to her,
she understood he came as Trinity.
How can I get my mind around that?
How can I get my mind's eye around that?

Based on Chapter 4

Julian also saw Mary, the mother of our Lord, in a spiritual vision. She saw her as a simple, humble young woman who was able to say 'yes' to God; who stands second only to Christ as the greatest of God's creatures.

This was followed by another showing:

Our good Lord showed me spiritually how intimate (homely) is his love. He is at hand to help us in a good, comforting way. He is our clothing – he wraps us around, encircling us in a loving embrace to shelter and surround us in a tender, steadfast love. So I perceived in this sight that he is everything that I understand as good.

Chapter 5

Then she was shown

something small, no bigger than a hazelnut, lying in the palm of my hand, as it seemed to me, and it was as round as a ball. I looked at it with the eye of my understanding and thought: What can this be?

Colledge & Walsh, Chapter 5, page 183

5

Then, resting in this reassurance,
Julian saw something else,
something small and insignificant.
She saw, in the palm of her hand,
   something as small as a hazelnut,
    as round as a ball.
So small, so frail,
  how could it last?
   What could it be?
And then the answer came –
It lasts because God made it,
  and he protects it;
   but more than that,
    God loves it.
Everything has its being through God's love,
  all of creation –
   and you and me.

Based on Chapter 5

What can this mean for us today? Think of the way in which scientists tell us how the world began. Our universe started in 'a point of time' or a 'particularity' and exploded into being, in what we call 'The Big Bang'. Julian's hazelnut, the tiniest thing, could be seen as symbolic of that. Later Julian also sees 'God in a point'. It may also bring to mind Paul's words to the Philippians that Jesus emptied himself of everything to become a human being.

As Julian saw
the whole vast universe
contracted to the
preposterously small ball
lying in the palm of her hand –

the size of a hazelnut,
just so our vast God
contracted himself to the
preposterously small being
born on this earth,
the same as you and me.

Based on Chapter 5

The hazelnut also says to us that our God cares, no matter how small we consider ourselves. Our mighty God is also familiar (homely), and he is the one for whom our heart yearns.

A Prayer

God, in your goodness, give me yourself,
for you are all I long for and need.
Anything less would not be enough –
I would always be conscious of want.
Only in you do I find everything.
Amen.

Based on Chapter 5

Meditation 3

Prayer and Contemplation

But whenever you pray, go into your room and shut the door and pray to your Father who is in secret; and your Father who sees in secret will reward you. When you are praying, do not heap up empty phrases as the Gentiles do; for they think that they will be heard because of their many words. Do not be like them, for your Father knows what you need before you ask him.

Matthew 6.6–8

Julian lived in a feudal age where the chasm between the nobility and peasants was vast and unbridgeable. The rule of law was dependent on the king and his courtiers. If you could find someone who had the king's ear to plead your cause in any dispute, you had a chance of being successful. This situation was transferred to the heavenly courts. It was accepted that you brought your petition before the King of kings through an intermediary who was close to him. Christ's mother was the most popular.

We mostly see Jesus today as our friend who walks life's journey with us and who is there to listen to our prayers, although many Christians also pray through the saints or Mary. This would have been the way that Julian was taught to pray, but she breaks with custom as she comes to see a different image of God. She sees that even if we pray through 'Christ's holy flesh, his passion, his death or wounds, the Holy Cross, or the saints' (Chapter 6), and even if we pray through Mary, it all ultimately comes from the goodness of God.

This showing was given so that we understand how wise it is to rely on the goodness of God. At the same time I was reminded of our habits of prayer: how because of ignorance of love, we pray through many intermediaries. Then I saw that truly it gives God more honour and delight if we faithfully pray to him for his goodness, and stick to this by grace with true understanding and steadfast belief than if we used every intermediary that we could think of. For even if we pray through all these intermediaries, it is still not enough to honour God completely. His goodness, however, is full and complete. It lacks nothing.

Chapter 6

Julian came to realize that she can approach God directly – she had no need of any intermediary.

Not as a lowly subject
who petitions the king
through a courtier;
not as a litigant
who petitions the judge
through his advocate;
not as a worker
who petitions his boss
through the shop-floor steward;
but as a child
who runs to his father and mother directly
can we come before God –
for the highest prayer
is to trust in his goodness,
which encompasses all our needs,

enlivens our very being
and enfolds us in love.

Based on Chapter 6

Julian calls her showings 'a lesson of love' and says that the reason she was given them was to help Christians in spiritual contemplation of God in order that they may know and love him more. This makes the soul (person) seem less in their own eyes, fills them with reverent fear for God and with greater love for their fellow Christians (Chapter 6). In short:

Contemplating God,
my ego diminishes;
Love for others grows.

A Haiku based on Chapter 6

A Prayer

God, you are all goodness, yet you love us as we are, longing for goodness and never attaining it.

Give us the assurance that you are here with us, so that we may have your 'grace and help to persevere in spiritual contemplation'.

May we know and love you more, as well as our fellow men and women, till we possess you in the fullness of joy. Amen.

Meditation 4

Experiencing the Passion

It was nine o'clock in the morning when they crucified him. The inscription of the charge against him read, 'The King of the Jews.' And with him they crucified two bandits, one on his right and one on his left. Those who passed by derided him, shaking their heads and saying, 'Aha! You who would destroy the temple and build it in three days, save yourself, and come down from the cross!' In the same way the chief priests, along with the scribes, were also mocking him among themselves and saying, 'He saved others; he cannot save himself. Let the Messiah, the King of Israel, come down from the cross now, so that we may see and believe.' Those who were crucified with him also taunted him.

Mark 15.25–32

Julian's century, the fourteenth, was one of violence and death. It saw the assassination of a king and an archbishop. The Black Death ravaged the country more than once. The peasants revolted and were cruelly suppressed. Even the Church was not spared – the monasteries were degenerating, the Pope was in exile in Avignon, reform was repressed and heresy suspected. England had just embarked on a war with France that would last for a hundred years.

It sounds much like our century but, in a manner unknown to Julian, the images of our violent and broken society are brought right into our living rooms through television. We can even see a modern rendition of the crucifixion on cinema screens, but does this lead us to experience the Passion in any meaningful way? It is regarded by many as merely a spectacle and we shy away from thinking of Christ's blood flowing for us. Julian, though, longed to 'experience the Passion as though she were present'. She was granted this wish and it brought her real pain. Yet even in the midst of this she experienced great joy.

For our courteous Lord showed his Passion to me in five ways,
first is the bleeding of the head,
second the discolouration of his blessed face,
third is the copious bleeding of the body in the furrows made by the scourging,
fourth is the deep drying –
these four ways were for the suffering of Christ in his Passion –
and the fifth is this – which was revealed for the joy and bliss of the Passion.

Colledge & Walsh, Chapter 23, page 218

Jesus hanging on the cross;
the crown of thorns still pressed into his head,
the sun hot and dry.
Nails tearing his hands and feet,
blood running down his forehead:
drops of blood, gushing like rain
from the eaves in a downpour,
drying to brown on his cheeks,
living and vivid,
hideous and cruel,
yet sweet and lovely,
full of beauty and joy.

For in this death there is life,
in this suffering, joy,
in this hideous act,
the turning point of history:
and Christ who is highest and noblest,
mightiest and most honourable,
is also lowest and humblest,
and graciously our friend.

Based on Chapter 7

The vision affected Julian deeply and she pondered its meaning as she was shown more vividly Christ's agony and loss
of blood. She saw that blood flowing for the redemption of
humankind.

Being 'washed in the blood of the Lamb'
is a phrase from the past.
To us now it is distasteful,
  melodramatic,
    over the top.
We avoid talk of Christ's blood,
  his blood shed for us;
we, who are confronted daily,
  in our living rooms,
    with pictures of a broken and bleeding world.
Julian saw Christ bleeding copiously
  from his scourging –
    his blood flowing freely, flowing all around,
      continuing to flow,
        flowing over and around her.
And she saw the power of that blood,
Christ's precious and plentiful blood,

descending into Hell and breaking its bond,
   ascending into Heaven, in the body of Christ,
     praying for us;
his blood, so precious and plentiful.

Based on Chapter 12

How often do you feel overwhelmed by the violence you experience, either directly or through the media? Julian must have
witnessed or been told about the violence and suffering that was
rife in her time as well. But she didn't let this overwhelm her. She
held in her mind the Passion of Jesus, where victory over all the
forces of evil was won, and this gave her strength.

A Prayer

Do any memories of violence, wounding or bleeding haunt
you? Is there anything redemptive in them? Bring them to
Christ to be transformed. Pray for that precious and plentiful blood to wash clean your memories, your spirit, your
very self, and to fill you with joy.

Meditation 5

Searching and Seeing

Ask, and it will be given you; search, and you will find; knock, and the door will be opened for you. For everyone who asks receives, and everyone who searches finds, and for everyone who knocks, the door will be opened.

Matthew 7.7–8

Part of our human nature is to be constantly longing for something more. What are you looking for in your relationship with God? Are you searching for a greater commitment, a deeper understanding, a steadier faith? What we often forget is that God is searching for us, wanting to show us more, surrounding us with his presence. But often, just as we feel we are finding something, we lose it again.

Julian found this to be true. In the second of her showings, she saw Christ's bleeding face as he hung on the cross, in what she calls a 'bodily vision' – we might use the phrase 'in virtual reality' today.

This I saw bodily, fearfully and faintly and I wanted more daylight to see it more clearly and the answer came to my mind. If God wishes to show you more he will be your light; you need no other but him. For I saw him and still searched for him, for we are now so blind and foolish that we can never search for God until he in his goodness shows himself to us. And when by grace we catch a glimpse of him, the same grace moves us with a great desire to see him more perfectly. So I saw him and sought him, and I had him and lacked him; and this is and should be our ordinary undertaking in this life, as I see it.

Chapter 10

And so it is, I'm sure for you as it is for me.

> I seek and I find,
> but I find I have found nothing,
> and I need to keep on seeking.

> I look and see and then I perceive
> I am seeing only the dark,
> and I need to keep on looking.

> I lack and I possess,
> but I find I possess a shadow,
> and I need to keep on striving to possess.
> But this is, and should be,
> our ordinary way of being in this life.

Based on Chapter 10

Julian reminds us that though we were created in God's image, and sin has spoilt that image, God in his love wishes to restore it. As we were made like him, God wishes us to be like Christ in our re-making, and so we continually search for him with the gifts that he gives us.

> All our life we search for a fullness that we never find.
> All our life we see, but never fully comprehend.
> It is God who draws us on – and gives us three gifts –

that we willingly seek him, diligently and happily, with his grace;

that we faithfully wait for him, lovingly and without complaining;
that we have great trust in him, out of complete and true faith.

For he will come to us and he will be fully seen,
For he is very accessible, very close, and he cares.

Based on Chapter 10

Julian came to see that:

Our soul's continual searching pleases God greatly, for we cannot do more than search, suffer and trust. And this comes to fulfilment in everyone to whom it is given by the Holy Spirit. Through the Spirit's grace, when it is his will, finding brings enlightenment. Our searching with faith, hope and love pleases our Lord, and finding pleases us and fills us with joy . . . It is God's will that we go on searching until we see him.

Chapter 10

A Prayer

Lord, I am impatient and easily discouraged. I want instant answers to my prayers. I long to see you now. Give me patience. Open my eyes to really see what you are revealing to me at this time. If I lose that again, give me perseverance and your grace. Help me to keep on searching for you, to bear with any suffering this causes and never to stop trusting in you. Amen.

Meditation 6

God Does Everything

Then Job answered the LORD: *'I know that you can do all things, and that no purpose of yours can be thwarted.'*

Job 42.1–2

When things go wrong in our lives, and sometimes they go horribly wrong, while we try to pick up the pieces and put them together again, we search for answers. We cry out, 'Why, Lord?' We ask, 'Where were you, God, when this happened?' and 'Why didn't you prevent it?' We try to hang on to Paul's promise that 'all things work together for good for those who love God' (Romans 8.28), but we walk mostly in a fog of incomprehension. We encounter the conundrum that plagued Julian and countless others through the ages. If God is all good and he does everything, how can there be evil? This is one of the chief problems that many people say prevent them from believing in a loving God.

In Julian's third showing she sees a vision of God:

> After this I saw God in a split second (in a point), meaning I saw him in my understanding. In this showing I saw that God is present in all things. I thought deeply about this and came to the realization that God does everything that is done.
>
> *Chapter 11*

Her response is to marvel at this, but also to ask 'What about sin?' And we add: What about evil? What about natural disasters that bring so much suffering? Are those God's doing?

Julian waits and is shown that God does what he does from his foreseeing wisdom. He knows long before and guides the outcome of events. When something happens suddenly, from our restricted vision we call it 'bad luck or good luck', but God acts out of love. So Julian concludes that everything is well done, right and complete, not as we think – some done well, some badly.

She says her 'soul was examined, powerfully, wisely and lovingly in this vision, and I saw that I really must agree, with great reverence and joy in God' (Chapter 11).

Julian struggled through to some sort of resolution, but what about us? Can we accept things the same way she did? Does this offer any clarity in the fog of incomprehension?

Julian longed to see God –
and in an instant of time she did.
She saw that he is present in all things,
and she saw that he does everything that is done.

Seeing God in this way made her wonder –
What about sin?
What about all the evil in our world?
What about all that is not right?
These are our self-same wonders.

Julian saw truly that God does
everything that is done –
and he does it in his foreseeing wisdom;
there is no such thing as chance,
no such thing as good or bad luck.
For she saw that God leads events
to their best end,
and God does no evil.

He does not sin.
In fact sin is no deed,
it is no thing.

Julian found this hard –
she wondered at it.
She saw that God was testing her in this sight.
She saw that she needed to assent,
and she happily did so.
I find this hard.
I still wonder at it.
I still don't see that God does what we call evil.
So I don't see that God does everything that is done.

Both her way and my way leave questions,
leave so many unanswered questions.

Based on Chapter 11

Indeed, so many unanswered questions. We just have to live with them and the insights that come to us from time to time, as we continue to search for understanding in God's grace, with Julian's help.

A Prayer

Dear Lord, I have so many questions, so much I do not understand about the way things are in my life. Help me to stay with you, to trust that you have had everything in your control from the beginning and that it is all good. May I continue to walk with my hand in yours, believing that one day I will see things more clearly. Amen.

Meditation 7

Overcoming the Fiend

The seventy returned with joy, saying, 'Lord, in your name
even the demons submit to us!' He said to them, 'I watched
Satan fall from heaven like a flash of lightning.'
                                                    Luke 10.17–18

Julian continued, as we do, to wrestle with the whole problem
of evil. If Christ's death overcame evil then why is there still so
much in the world? We, by and large, discount the image of evil
personalized as the Devil or Satan or the Evil One. If anything,
we talk of evil as some amorphous power. Julian believed in the
Devil, calling him the 'Fiend'. She writes of her fifth showing:

> With this the fiend is overcome. Our Lord said this to me
> with reference to his blessed Passion, as he had shown it
> before. In this he showed a part of the fiend's malice, and all
> of his impotence, because he showed that his Passion is the
> overcoming of the fiend. God showed me that the fiend has
> now the same malice as he had before the Incarnation, and
> he works as hard, and he sees as constantly as he did before
> that all souls who will be saved escape him to God's glory by
> the power of our Lord's precious Passion.
>   *Colledge & Walsh, Chapter 13, page 201*

Julian goes beyond seeing that the Fiend is overcome and rejoices
in his impotence.

Our world is still awash
with suffering, oppression, violence.
The dark forces of Satan hold sway;
the Fiend is hard at work;
the world is in his power.

But look again, look deeply,
at the man on the cross;
his blood copiously flowing;
his slow and agonizing death –
but not the triumph of evil.

For with this the Fiend is overcome!
With this dawns the great reversal.
He still works as hard as before, with the same malice,
but now all that God permits him to do
turns to joy for us and to sorrow and shame for him.

For those who see with the eye of faith
see the Fiend frustrated at his impotence,
for his power is locked in God's hands,
and all the hurt and evil he causes us
will be changed into our eternal joy.

Based on Chapter 13

At the thought that the Devil (Fiend), who was such a fearful creature, is now scorned by God, Julian laughed out loud, causing those with her to join in. This is another instance of her breaking new ground, and in two ways: firstly in seeing that the Devil, a figure who evoked so much fear in her society, is actually a frustrated scorned figure, and secondly that Christians can actually laugh and be merry, 'I understood that we may laugh, to comfort ourselves and rejoice in God, because the Fiend is overcome' (Chapter 13).

Dark and sombre the mood,
mother and siblings hovering,
wiping her fevered brow with cool cloths;
the priest holding aloft the crucifix
on which her eyes are fixed,
all watching for her last breath,
while longing for the next laboured one,
and the next . . .

When, suddenly, she laughs out loud,
so merrily, so spontaneously,
that they all are infected and
all of them burst out laughing.
In a moment the room is awash
with waves of mirth, death forgotten,
life ascending.

Hushing again as Julian talks,
for this needs some explaining:
'By this the Fiend is overcome',
she proclaims, turning her gaze again
on the crucifix, 'by Christ's Passion,
by his blood pouring out so plentifully'.
We can laugh at the Devil,
that poor impotent creature,
and scorn him as nothing,
while we still seriously oppose
whatever he tries to do.

Based on Chapter 13

I'm sure neither you nor I usually feel like laughing at the Devil, but rather, the questions keep on coming – questions about suffering, about the Devil's power and about whether he has really been conquered.

A Prayer

Lord, help me to understand and accept that indeed the Fiend is overcome. Help me to see what it is you have done, and to trust in what you are doing right now. Help me to find joy and cause for laughter in you in the midst of temptation, pain and suffering. Amen.

Meditation 8

Reward in Heaven

When they heard these things, they became enraged and ground their teeth at Stephen. But filled with the Holy Spirit, he gazed into heaven and saw the glory of God and Jesus standing at the right hand of God. 'Look,' he said, 'I see the heavens opened and the Son of Man standing at the right hand of God!' But they covered their ears, and with a loud shout all rushed together against him. Then they dragged him out of the city and began to stone him.

Acts 7.54–58a

Our view of the earth is so different from Julian's as well as from that of Jesus and his friends; for one, we see it as only part of a whole universe. This makes our concept of heaven much more problematic. How do you imagine heaven? After being shown that Satan or the Fiend has indeed been overcome, Julian is shown, in her next revelation, how God rewards his faithful servants:

After this our Lord said: 'Thank you for your service and the labour of your youth.' At that I was lifted up to heaven in my imagination, where I saw our Lord God as a lord in his own house, hosting all his friends to a splendid feast. I did not see him take any special seat although he reigned as a king, but he was present in the whole house, filling it with laughter and personally putting each guest at ease, in a familiar (homely) and respectful (courteous) way, with a joyous expression like

25

a melody of love. The same expression fills all heaven with the joy and happiness of the divinity.

Chapter 14

Is this how you envisage heaven? It is one of the most mysterious places to try and imagine.

I wonder too about heaven –
Are those who die in the faith there already?
Do they know and meet each other?
What do they do all the time?
Gather around a throne with their harps
and sing all day?
Not my idea of a good time:
not what I want to do for Eternity.

Julian was shown a glimpse of heaven
and she saw our Lord God
calling his friends to a feast,
filling his house full of joy and mirth,
being there himself as a close friend
to gladden and console us,
thanking us each one for coming,
and radiating his joy and bliss
to everyone forever.
That sounds more like heaven.

Based on Chapter 14

The thought of heaven and what it is like became more urgent for me when we recently lost our son, Steve, suddenly and tragically. What is he doing now? Is he in heaven? Where and what is that actually?

Asking Steve about Heaven

You have left us and gone on,
but gone on to where?
To heaven where you join the saints
gathered around God's throne
singing praises without end?
Have you walked from room to room
in the house of many mansions,
and found your forebears, old friends
and those you always wanted to meet?

Is it better than here –
even though here was good to you?
Is it tinged with sadness
by the absence and grieving
of those you left behind
or have you forgotten them in your rejoicing?

Where have you gone?
Gone to some place
where we will meet you again?
Or have you gone to some huge Waiting Room,
with a multitude of others,
milling around,
impatient with inactivity,
thinking that if this is heaven you want out?

Where have you gone?
Into nothingness?
A black hole?
Is this all there is in the afterwards –
Oblivion?
Is heaven just a big con?

Stephen, killed for his faith;
as he died, he saw heaven open –
God in his glory and Jesus at his side.
John, exiled for his faith;
he too saw heaven open.
Did you see it as you left?
Left with no return, unlike Paul,
lifted into the third heaven,
who returned to tell of it.

Where have you gone?
Did Jesus meet you?
What are you doing?
Is it really heaven there?
One day, one day,
we will join you.
One day we will know:
look out for us.

We can exercise our imagination, but in the end, we have no way of knowing, and must live in this world by faith, trusting in God's promises about the next. And we can take reassurance from Scripture and also from Julian, who was shown 'three degrees of bliss' (Chapter 14) coming to those who serve God. We will receive honour and thanks from God, and everyone will see this honour and thanks, and our joy at first being received in heaven will last forever.

A Prayer

Lord, help me to live day by day, serving and honouring you in all I do in this world and leaving the next in your good hands together with those who have gone before. Amen.

Meditation 9

Swinging Between Well and Woe

For everything there is a season, and a time for every matter
under heaven:
a time to be born, and a time to die;
a time to plant, and a time to pluck up what is planted;
a time to kill, and a time to heal;
a time to break down, and a time to build up;
a time to weep, and a time to laugh;
a time to mourn, and a time to dance.

Ecclesiastes 3.1–4

If we have a feeling of well-being, we can face whatever comes, but a feeling of gloom and pessimism makes us reluctant to tackle anything. Are these feelings always dependent on outward circumstances or do they sometimes come from within? After her vision of heaven Julian tells us that she felt elated, as we would expect:

And after this he showed me within my soul the most wonderful spiritual delight. This filled me with unending certainty, so that I felt powerfully protected without any painful fear. This feeling so filled my spirit with joy and peace that I was totally sure that nothing on earth could shake me.

This lasted only for a while, and then I was changed. I felt myself abandoned, in such sadness and weariness of life and so fed up with myself that I hardly had the patience to go on living.

Chapter 15

We could put it this way:

Yesterday was a rainbow day,
a gemstone day, that shouted,
'Look at me!'
I knew I had those things
in me that meant
I could produce
something of worth –
  imagination,
    skill,
      an inner sight,
to plum the mysteries of the universe
and put them on display.

Foolish indeed!
Today is heavy,
  grey and flat,
    a dark and dreary day,
and I can hear a scornful voice
that whispers,
  'Just where did you get such vain ideas?'
For all has drained away
  and left a woeful emptiness
    I struggle to express.

Based on Chapter 15

Isn't this an experience on our spiritual journey that we have all been through? The times of exaltation after something wonderful has happened, but then it all seems to disappear and we are left questioning our very faith. We feel with Julian:

My spirit soared as
I felt the presence of God,
his powerful protection
and his peace.
It was well with my soul.

But in a moment this had gone;
for God abandoned me,
and, weary and depressed,
I had no wish to go on living.
My soul was overwhelmed by woe.

And like a yo-yo
I plunged up and down:
from well to woe,
from woe to well;
from joy to pain
and back again.

Was the joy my doing?
Did I deserve God's presence?
Was the pain my fault?
Did I cause God's absence?

No – sometimes joy bursts
in on us as sheer gift.
Sometimes, without cause,
sorrow overwhelms us. But

in well or in woe, God is still present.
Pain will pass and joy will last.
Hold on to that.

Based on Chapter 15

Julian came to understand that God was showing her that sometimes we are not directly responsible for feeling either up or down, well or woe. We should accept both with equanimity and know that God is with us in love whatever our moods.

For it is God's will that we do all in our power to maintain our well-being, for joy lasts forever, and pain passes, and will come to naught for those who will be saved. So it is not God's will that when we feel pain we should make a thing of it in sorrow and mourning, but rather we should quickly pass it over, and keep ourselves in the endless delight that is God.

Chapter 15

A Prayer

Good Lord, help me to depend on you and your word and not on my moods or feelings. In my upbeat moods, may I rejoice in your goodness and give you the praise. In my depressions, give me the strength to resist the way in which they drag me down, and the wisdom to seek outside help if necessary, while always relying on your goodness and grace. Amen.

Meditation 10

Pain

*Since therefore Christ suffered in the flesh, arm yourselves
also with the same intention (for whoever has suffered in
the flesh has finished with sin), so as to live for the rest of
your earthly life no longer by human desires but by the will
of God.*

1 Peter 4.1–2

How do we measure pain? By its intensity? By the length of time it
endures? By its nature, its cause and expected outcome? How do
we view the pain Christ suffered on the cross? Crucifixion is a most
horrific way to die, but have not others endured the same or worse?

Julian experienced the last moments of Christ on the cross and
saw his body drying up and his intense pain. She writes:

This revelation of Christ's pain filled me with pain. I know that
he suffered 'once for all', but as I had wished to experience his
suffering, he allowed me to do so. I felt no pain but Christ's
pain. When I had asked I had no idea what the pain would be
like. And now, in experiencing it, like a wretch, I regretted asking. It seemed to me that my pains were worse than any death,
and I thought, 'Is there any pain in hell like this pain?' and the
answer came to mind, 'Hell is a different pain, for in it there is
despair.' But of all the pains that lead to salvation, this is the
greatest, to see the lover suffer.

Chapter 17

I think of your pain, Lord,
the pain you bore for me –
no one could have borne more pain.
You carried the sins of the world.
Is the pain of hell not worse than your pain?
The pain of hell is a different pain,
for in it there is despair.

And the pain of realizing
how much hurt I have caused?
Or the pain and wretchedness I feel
when, by my words and actions,
I increase the suffering of others –
whether intended or unintended –
and I see just how rotten I am?
Lord, you never knew that pain.

The pain of the sinner is a different pain,
for in it there is regret and anguish.
Lord, you knew the pain of the victim,
never the pain of the perpetrator
who sees what he has done.

But did you become yourself a perpetrator?
Did all the anguish and regret
and despair of all the inflictors
and perpetrators of pain become yours?
Did that all bear down upon you,
crowding into your very being
till there was no room for God,
and you felt forsaken?

Pain

Does that pain cover all of our pain?
Does that pain heal our wretchedness,
lift us up from where we have fallen?
And because we go on falling
we can never stop grieving and weeping,
searching and yearning
for wholeness in you,
till you take all our pain into yourself.

Based on Chapters 17, 20, 72

It all became too much to bear, and Julian wanted to turn her gaze away from the cross and Christ's suffering, towards heaven.

There is so much suffering,
for so many, for so long:
it disturbs us, depresses us,
threatens to suck us into its black depths.

Julian felt the same,
for she saw the suffering of Christ
on the cross,
bleeding from his wounds,
his body drying,
becoming discoloured,
as his lifeblood drained out.

She saw too how pain was heaped on pain,
when he was abandoned
even by his father,
left standing alone.

It became too much to bear,
and she wanted to look away,
to look to heaven
for there was safety
and an end to grief.
But she did not.

She chose to keep on looking at Christ,
staying with his suffering.
So she came to see that
Christ was her heaven,
and the joy that came later
came only because she stayed her gaze
on the crucified Christ.

Based on Chapter 19

A Prayer

Think of the pain that you are bearing at this time. It may be a physical pain; it may be the sort of pain that goes on and on, the pain of loneliness, rejection, broken relation-ships; or it may be on behalf of loved ones who are in pain. In addition you may feel the suffering and brokenness of the world weighing you down. Bring whatever it is before Christ crucified and keep your gaze on him.

Meditation 11

Joy in Pain

*Sing praises to the LORD, O you his faithful ones, and give
thanks to his holy name.*
*For his anger is but for a moment; his favour is for a lifetime.
Weeping may linger for the night, but joy comes with the
morning.*
*You have turned my mourning into dancing; you have taken
off my sackcloth and clothed me with joy, so that my soul
may praise you and not be silent. O LORD my God, I will give
thanks to you for ever.*

Psalm 30.4–5, 11–12

Our natural inclination is to avoid pain and painful situations. But
pain is a warning to us that something is not right and needs attention, be it physical, emotional or spiritual. Pain is not good, but we
cannot ignore it. We need to deal with it, but how? We saw how
Julian discovered that it helped to keep her gaze on Christ suffering
on the cross, though she was tempted to turn her eyes away:

And I watched with all my might for the moment when
Christ would expire, and I expected to see his body quite
dead; but I did not see him so, and just at the moment when
by appearances it seemed to me that life could last no longer,
and that the revelation of his end must be near, suddenly,
as I looked at the same cross, he changed to an appearance
of joy. The change in his blessed appearance changed mine,
and I was as glad and joyful as I could possibly be. And then

cheerfully our Lord suggested to my mind: Where is there
now any instant of your pain or of your grief? And I was
very joyful . . .

Colledge & Walsh, Chapter 21, page 214

In the darkness of my pain,
in the night-time of my tears,
I turn and look at the cross;
I see Christ suffer, right to the death;
I wait for the dawn –
to bring resurrection,
hope, joy.

Julian waited – suffering
as she saw Christ suffer,
waited for his death –
but suddenly, all at one time,
his face lit up with joy!
She caught the radiance –
it filled her with joy –
made her as glad and joyful
as she could possibly be.
It was joy in the midst of pain,
easing it, transforming it,
making it bearable.

Still Christ suffered, still Christ died.
He suffered to make us heirs
with him of his joy.
Still we suffer, still we die,
but our suffering can bring its rewards,
can lead us into deeper unity with Christ,

can be transformed, all at one time,
into joy –
making us as glad and as joyful
as we can possibly be.

Based on Chapter 21

Of course we know that the end of all our pain and the coming
of true joy will only happen when Christ brings in his kingdom,
and all our pains will be turned into rewards. But I'm sure you
know, as I do, men and women who suffer greatly yet still radiate
a wonderful Christian joy. Pain and joy, suffering and triumph
can co-exist.

We do need to accept what Christ is offering us, and Julian is
shown next that it does matter to him whether we accept or not.
'We are his joy, and he finds endless delight in us, and so with his
grace we shall delight in him' (Chapter 23).

Because Jesus finds joy in giving us salvation and is delighted
when we respond with joy, Julian was reminded of the qualities
of a cheerful giver. And the joy in giving and receiving is thus
multiplied, and reduces our pain.

A friend gave me a gift,
a gift of value and beauty.
She gave it to please me,
and to comfort me,
and because I received it
gladly and gratefully
she was glad too, and
all her expense and labour
fell away as nothing,
because of my delight.

But if she had given a gift
to please me and comfort me;
if I had looked at it
and found it wanting,
or paid it little heed,
she would be sad, but more
than sad, be hurt,
and this would form
a rift between us.

Just so is Christ joyful
if we accept his gift
of love and life,
given at great cost,
and immeasurably sad
if we reject him.

Based on Chapter 23

A Prayer

Lord, help me bring my pain,
the pain of those I love, and even the pain of the world,
to the foot of your cross as I keep my gaze on you:
not to wallow in it, and not to ignore it,
but to work through it,
so that it can be changed into redemption and joy.
Help me not to be overwhelmed by pain.
Help me not to despair.
Help me to see that you are always there,
holding out your gifts of love and grace,
and in the midst of it all, of joy.
Amen.

Meditation 12

Seeing Things Differently

A week later his disciples were again in the house, and Thomas was with them. Although the doors were shut, Jesus came and stood among them and said, 'Peace be with you.' Then he said to Thomas, 'Put your finger here and see my hands. Reach out your hand and put it in my side. Do not doubt but believe.' Thomas answered him, 'My Lord and my God!' Jesus said to him, 'Have you believed because you have seen me? Blessed are those who have not seen and yet have come to believe.'

John 20.26–29

The way we express our Christian faith today varies greatly from place to place and denomination to denomination, and even within denominations; a word that Julian would not have known. She only knew of 'Holy Church' and the way in which Christians were expected to view and practise their faith. We have more freedom today, and such variety, that some practices of other Christians may seem strange and unappealing to us. Christians also differ greatly in the regard and position that they give to Mary, the mother of Jesus. There are also different ways that the death of Jesus is viewed, from graphic pictures of the crucifixion to the barest, plainest cross. Julian records how Jesus showed her the wounds in his side and his heart split in two:

With a face full of kindness our good Lord looked into his side, and as he gazed his joyful and sweet expression drew my understanding into this same wound in his side. And there

41

he revealed a lovely and delightful place, large enough for all of humankind that will be saved, and will rest in peace and love . . . And in this sweet sight he showed his blessed heart split in two.

Chapter 24

The next showing followed swiftly:

But with this same expression of mirth and joy, our good Lord looked down towards his right and brought to my mind where our Lady stood at the time of his Passion. And he said, 'Do you wish to see her?'

Chapter 25

When Julian answered in the affirmative, she was shown, not a physical likeness as she expected, but a spiritual vision of Mary:

Whereas before I had seen her small and simple, now I was shown her exalted and noble and glorious and more pleasing to him than all others. And so he wishes it to be known that all who take delight in him should take delight in her, as well as in the delight that he has in her and she in him.

Chapter 25

Julian saw two images,
popular among the pious,
both then and now:
Christ's heart split in two,
in sorrow at our sins;
and his mother – the humble maid
become the Queen of Heaven,
crowned and robed in glory.

Julian saw the same two images,
but she saw something else –
wider, deeper, brighter:
cheerfully and joyfully she was shown
Christ's heart split in two,
how he suffered for her, yes,
but how it has now all turned to joy and mirth;
how Jesus delights in giving this joy to us.

Still in mirth and joy,
Jesus showed his mother,
not her beauty,
but her virtues –
simple and humble,
full of truth,
wisdom, love,
through which Julian herself
should learn to know herself
and her Lord.

Julian was shown as well
how she is raised to the heights,
now radiating glory and joy,
because of her son's love for her.
Julian saw all this
and it filled her with delight.

Based on Chapters 24, 25

Julian saw these two things in many ways, as did her contemporaries, but she also saw something different in them. What do you see in them? Do they mean anything special to you? Could they, should they mean more to you?

Reflect on the way in which you have usually thought of the wound in Jesus' side and his own heartbreak. Ask for openness to see and experience something different in this. Reflect on the way in which you regard Mary. Has it been largely with neglect and reluctance to elevate her to any place as 'Queen of Heaven' because that has not been within your tradition? Or has it been to place her high above all other mortals, because that is how you were brought up to see her? Ask for openness to see and experience something different in this.

A Prayer

Oh Lord, help me not to be so set in my ways that I close myself off to new ways of seeing and understanding my faith and how I live it out day by day. Amen.

Meditation 13

Seeing God and Seeing Sin

But you are doing away with the fear of God, and hinder-
ing meditation before God. For your iniquity teaches your
mouth, and you choose the tongue of the crafty. Your own
mouth condemns you, and not I; your own lips testify
against you.

Job 15.4–6

Have you ever thought, when you look around you and see all
that is wrong and destructive in the way people treat each other,
'If only God had kept evil out of the world when he created it', or
'If only he had made us less prone to sin, wouldn't it be a much
better place?' Have you then gone on to try and work out why
God did allow evil in the world?

The same thoughts came to Julian, especially after she was shown
a vision of Jesus, now our Lord victorious in his majesty and power:

After this the Lord showed himself to me and he appeared
more glorified than I had seen him before. This was to teach
me that our souls will never find rest till they come to him,
acknowledging that he is joy in its fullness, intimate (homely)
and gracious (courteous), blissful and true life.

Chapter 26

The Lord said to her again and again,
I am he,

45

I am he who is highest.
I am he whom you love.
I am he in whom you delight.
I am he whom you serve.
I am he whom you desire.
I am he for whom you long.
I am he whom you intend.
I am he who is all.
I am he whom Holy Church preaches and teaches to you.
I am he who showed himself before to you.

These words filled her with a joy
greater than she could imagine
or her soul could ever desire.

Based on Chapter 26

But the reality of evil in our world kept on troubling her and she knew that without sin all would have been well. Why did God allow sin in the first place?

The Lord God made the heavens and the earth,
and every kind of creature and every kind of plant,
and he saw that it was good.
And the Lord God made man and woman
in his own image and gave them authority
over all that he had made,
and he saw that it was good.

The Lord God also made the serpent,
who was more crafty
than any other wild animal
that he had made,
and he let the serpent loose

in the world that he had made:
and so it was that sin entered the world.

Why, oh why, God, did you allow
the serpent to work his guile?
Why did you allow sin into your good world?
Without it nothing would stand between Christ and me;
without it there would have been no need
for Christ to suffer and to die;
without it all would have been well.

In answer Julian was shown an ugly sight –
all the pains that ever were or ever will be,
followed by the suffering and contempt and pain that
Christ endured –
far more than all the rest.
But she did not see sin –
sin as such –
only its effect:
she saw it has no kind of substance,
no share in being.

Sin is just there, real and inevitable,
and the cause of all the pain:
sin is us choosing our own way,
putting our selves at the centre,
tearing us apart, because this is not what we want –
if we long to be at one with Christ.

Julian was shown that
sin is inevitable,
sin is necessary,
given that we humans
were created with free will,

but she was also shown that,
though all now seems woeful,
all shall be well,
and all shall be well,
and all manner of things shall be well.

Based on Chapter 27

A Prayer

Dear Lord,

We believe that you are the creator of all that is, and that
you created and are still creating all in your wisdom and
love. We see a broken and suffering world. We see, along-
side the beauty of creation, violence, deprivation, hopeless-
ness. We see the sin of others and also our own sin, and we
despair.

Help us, Lord, to hold together with this picture that of
your suffering love. Help us to be energized by what you did
for us on the cross so that we can play our part in relieving
the suffering of others. Help us to cling to your promise that
'All shall be well', even when things appear far from well.
Give us vision, give us strength and give us grace. Amen.

Meditation 14

Who's to Blame?

If we say that we have no sin, we deceive ourselves, and the truth is not in us. If we confess our sins, he who is faithful and just will forgive us our sins and cleanse us from all unrighteousness. If we say that we have not sinned, we make him a liar, and his word is not in us.

1 John 1.8–10

When accused of any sort of wrongdoing, people usually react by denying the accusation, and if it is clear that they are responsible, they often try to put the blame on someone else. How true is this of you? I know this is what I do.

When things fall apart,
and the wheels come off,
we play the blaming game:
for it never is our fault.

The game goes way back
to the dawn of time,
when Adam first blamed Eve,
and Eve put the blame on the snake.

Children blame their parents;
workers blame the boss;
blacks blame whites and whites blame blacks,
while all agree it's the government's fault.

But we're all to blame
for the mess we've made,
and God knows this from the start.
Yet he looks at us with pity and love,
as if free of guilt as children,
and puts away all our blame.

Based on Chapter 28

When we do accept that we are to blame – that it was our sin that caused hurt and pain – we feel devastated and humiliated. We may even take more blame upon ourselves than is warranted.

Julian saw in this reaction three things that we should remember; first, that each suffering and humiliation will be turned to joy and honour; second, that Christ also suffers with us and his suffering surpasses ours; and third, that our sin deserves this pain anyway but in it God is not punishing us but being merciful.

He wants us to see that his pains and his tribulations are so much greater than we could ever suffer or even imagine. If we understand his will in this, it stops our grumbling and despairing as we experience our pains; and even if we acknowledge that our sins deserve them, his love still excuses us. In his graciousness (courtesy) he sets aside all our blame, and sees us in pity and compassion as innocent, guiltless children.

Chapter 28

She goes on to explain how God in Christ longs to do this for us, to set aside our blame, but he needs our response. She sees in the words of Jesus on the cross, 'I thirst', a deeper meaning:

Who's to Blame?

'I thirst', said Jesus from the cross,
as his lifeblood drained away,
and the noonday sun beat down on him.

'I thirst', said Jesus,
and he says it still, for his love and pity
make him thirst and yearn
for each one of us to return his love.

And the power of this yearning in Christ
enables us to respond,
for it draws us to himself,
and to his joy.

Based on Chapter 31

A Prayer

Lord, help me to see those areas in my life that are wrong, and in seeing them and the hurt they have caused and how I go on and on failing you, myself and others, help me not to sink into a black pit of blame and shame, but to turn to you.

Help me truly to see that you are looking at me with pity and compassion and to leave myself in your hands.

Lord, if on the other hand I feel that I'm doing alright, and start to feel complacent, show me those areas of my life that need changing, and help me to do so, for the sake of Jesus Christ, our Lord. Amen.

Meditation 15

All Shall Be Well

*He is the head of the body, the church; he is the beginning,
the firstborn from the dead, so that he might come to have
first place in everything. For in him all the fullness of God
was pleased to dwell, and through him God was pleased
to reconcile to himself all things, whether on earth or in
heaven, by making peace through the blood of his cross.*

Colossians 1.18–20

Julian must surely be known most of all for the familiar phrase
as 'All shall be well, and all shall be well and all manner of thing
shall be well'. 'All shall be well', which is usually qouted in the
older English version. It has been used by other poets and writ-
ers and it may be this phrase that drew you to Julian's writings
in the first place. When was Julian first given this assurance?
And how did she react to it?

When Julian was depressed at the thought of her sin and how
it hindered her from getting closer to God, Jesus came to her and
assured her that, although sin was inevitable,

All shall be well,
and all shall be well
and all manner of thing shall be well.

Chapter 27

We treasure this traditional version of Julian's words, because if
we put the phrase into our current language it sounds trite and
loses its ring:

It will all be OK.
It will all be alright.
It will all come right in the end.

But put whichever way, the words bring reassurance – or do they? In the face of everything wrong that confronts us, how could things be OK in the end?

Here we are one with Julian, who cried out 'Ah, good Lord, how can all be well considering the great damage sin has brought upon your creation? . . . Here I wanted, as much as I dared, a more explicit explanation to put me at ease regarding this matter' (Chapter 29).

There are so many questions
that crowd around,
demanding attention.
For those that ask How?
What? and Who?
there are answers –
books, experts, the Internet,
the Bible and the Church.
How can I be saved?
What is our God like?
Which way should I follow?
The answers are open, bright,
clear and plentiful.
They bring joy and peace.

But there are other questions,
that needle us from deep within,
more persistent, more unsettling.
How can this be?

What does this mean?
What will happen?
And Why? Why? Why?
Why the world's suffering?
Why my own grief and suffering?
Why the intransigence of evil?
Why my own failings?
Why, Lord, Why?

For these there are no clear-cut answers.
God keeps them hidden and closed from us.
They are not for us to know,
and the more we pry,
the further we move from knowing.

Accept the knowing
that we should trust and rejoice in God.
Accept the not knowing.
Keep on trusting and rejoicing in God.

Based on Chapter 30

Julian found resolution, for she then writes that 'our good Lord replied to all the questions and doubts that I could raise' (Chapter 31). He reassured her that he would make all things well and he says the same to us, so if we say:

I feel depressed when I look at our world –
It is so full of violence.
God our parent says,
'I am able to make all things well.'

It is torn apart by hatred.
Jesus our Saviour says,
'I know how to make all things well.'

54

Disaster follows disaster.
The Holy Spirit says,
'I wish to make all things well.'

Evil rules the day.
God, three-in-one, replies,
'I shall make all things well',

There is so much suffering;
The blessed Trinity replies,
'You will see for yourself that
all manner of things shall be well.'

Let these words enclose you
in Christ's rest and peace.

Based on Chapter 31

A Prayer

Lord, there are so many questions that I wrestle with, so many mysteries that trouble me and some that threaten to derail my faith. Keep me on the right track, holding on to you and believing that, no matter how I understand things at the moment, you are in fact making all things well. Amen.

Meditation 16

Questions

So when they had come together, they asked him, 'Lord, is this the time when you will restore the kingdom to Israel?' He replied, 'It is not for you to know the times or periods that the Father has set by his own authority. But you will receive power when the Holy Spirit has come upon you; and you will be my witnesses in Jerusalem, in all Judea and Samaria, and to the ends of the earth.'

Acts 1.6–8

Some of us are content to accept what is given; we look at something, admire its beauty or are thankful that it does what it is made to do. Others are by nature full of questions. We want to take things apart and see how they work; we want to find out what it is that gives them beauty. We question what we are told and want to understand what is behind the obvious. Julian was one of the latter. She wrestles with this conundrum: if God is almighty, and if God is all-loving, why does he not prevent evil and suffering? How can he promise that good will result out of everything that happens to us?

As we see it, so many malignant deeds are done, causing so much harm, that it seems impossible to us that it could ever end in anything good. We grieve and mourn about this to the extent that we can find no rest in the joyful contemplation of our Lord as we ought to.

Chapter 32

Has this been your experience as well?

> The world is far from well.
> It is like a laden lorry
> hurtling unstoppable to its destruction.
> We are overwhelmed by
> violence breeding violence,
> hatred setting one against the other,
> ugliness, decay, death,
> sorrow upon sorrow:
> and in the end hell and damnation –
> except for those who will be saved.
> How could it all be well?
> How could it possibly be well?
>
> *Based on Chapter 32*

Julian kept on coming back to this issue, so we will look at how she wrestled with it in the next few meditations. She wanted answers and so do we, and God responded:

> He gave me understanding in two parts. One part is of our saviour and our salvation. This blessed part is open, clear, bright and plentiful, and all who are of good will are understood to be part of it. We are bound to this by God, and attracted, counselled and taught inwardly by the Holy Spirit, and outwardly by Holy Church, through the same grace. This is what our Lord wants us to be engaged in, finding joy in him, as he finds joy in us.

> The other part, all that is additional to our salvation, is closed to us and hidden. It is our Lord's private counsel, and it is appropriate to his role as sovereign to keep it to himself,

and it is appropriate to our place as obedient and respectful servants not to wish to know his counsel.

Based on Chapter 30

As well as this word of caution, the words of reassurance that all would be well kept coming to Julian.

Yet these words came again and again:
'All shall be well,
all manner of thing shall be well;
I will make all things well.
This I reveal.
Rest in this and be at peace.
The how and when and what it is I will do
is not for you to know.'

Only stand firm in your faith,
and believe in our good Lord's love,
that he will make good his word
and will make well all that is not well.

Based on Chapter 32

Julian also came to realize that there were some things she would never understand, and in the end she should accept that she was never going to. But should we not try to understand all that we can?

A Prayer

I want to know, Lord.
You gave me a mind

that needs to know, an enquiring mind,
a logical mind that gathers facts,
sorting them and assessing them,
following through to conclusions.

But too many facts are elusive;
too many don't fit;
too often they lead nowhere;
too many mysteries remain.

Help me to use my mind to search,
to explore, to understand
what you wish to reveal.

But help me to know when I reach the point
where searching becomes speculation,
when I wander into those areas
you wish to conceal.

May I be content
whether you reveal or conceal,
and rest in your promise
that I am in your hands,
and all will be well.
Amen.

Based on Chapter 33

Meditation 17

All Shall Be Well – In the Face of Loss?

I consider that the sufferings of this present time are not worth comparing with the glory about to be revealed to us.

We know that all things work together for good for those who love God, who are called according to his purpose.

Romans 8.18, 28

What do we do in the face of a great personal tragedy or loss that shatters our lives? How do we go on living when the future looks utterly bleak and pointless? Most of us have experienced some kind of loss in our lives. Julian does not tell us in her writings of any great personal loss, neither do we know of any, although Father John-Julian in his recent book, *The Complete Julian of Norwich*, suggests that she might have had her illness and her showings in the same year as the traumatic, untimely death of her husband, after which she moved back to her family home (Fr John-Julian, page 24). She would almost certainly have experienced the loss of someone close to her as successive waves of the Black Death decimated the population, and famine and wars all added their toll. As we have seen, she questions, as we do, how in the face of all the evil things happening around her, any good could possibly come from them.

When the ordered tenor of our life
is shattered by the unimaginable;
when the phonecall that splinters
others' lives rings for us;
when a nightmare that horrifies
turns into reality,
how can we believe that
anything could be well again –
ever?

Anguish breaks over us in torrents,
like the torrents that overwhelmed you –
submerged you, extinguished your life.
But we surface again,
we go on living,
we face each day,
wounded and grieving.

We hold on to each other,
and take a halting step:
can we dare hope
that all shall be well,
and all shall be well,
and all manner of thing shall be well again –
ever?

Based on Chapter 32

These lines were written ten days after our eldest son, Steve, drowned while tubing down a river during a weekend away with his family. At a time like this, glib words of comfort and even friends quoting Scripture verses with the best intentions

61

are not at all helpful. 'All things work together for good' is hard to swallow, and 'All shall be well' is just as remote a possibility. I wrote months later:

Even with the passing of time,
even with the return to normal life,
our son is still absent,
but he comes suddenly in his absence;
sorrow and tears flooding in again.

Even with the passing of time,
the questions keep coming,
'Why him?' 'Why such a waste
of his talent and commitment?'
'What good could possibly come
from this and how?'

Even with the passing of time,
I still hear the words that Julian heard,
'All manner of thing shall be well'
and even, 'You will see for yourself
that every kind of thing will be well.'
Still they sound hollow and mocking.

But Julian wrestled with this too,
sorrowing and mourning restlessly,
till she came to see that it is
our own sight, which is so blinkered,
so wayward and feeble,
that prevents us from seeing
God's wisdom, power and goodness.

All we can do now is
to keep on walking in faith,
to carry with us our unanswered questions,

to wait for the day when all will become clear,
when we will see for ourselves
that all manner of thing shall be well.

Based on Chapter 32

Julian came to see that tragedy and suffering will inevitably come to Christians: 'Holy Church will be shaken in sorrow and tribulation in this world as men shake a cloth in the wind' (Chapter 28). We forget this and so despair when it happens to us.

And the cause is this: that the reasoning we use is now so blind, so pitiful and so inadequate that we cannot recognize God's superior, wonderful wisdom, or the power and the goodness of the blessed Trinity.

Based on Chapter 32

This being the case, it seemed impossible to me that well could come out of every kind of thing, as the Lord revealed to me at this time. And our Lord showed me no other answer except this: What is impossible to you, is not impossible to me. I shall keep my word in all things, and I shall make all well.

Based on Chapter 32

A Prayer

Lord, when I feel my loss so greatly that tears wash over me and words fail me and I feel I cannot go on, lift me and carry me through. Amen.

Meditation 18

All Shall Be Well – In the Face of Our Sin?

For while we were still weak, at the right time Christ died for the ungodly. Indeed, rarely will anyone die for a righteous person – though perhaps for a good person someone might actually dare to die. But God proves his love for us in that while we still were sinners Christ died for us.

Romans 5.6–8

Sin is not a very popular word or concept these days. A few centuries ago we would have been frightened into the kingdom of heaven by pictures of sinners being condemned for all eternity to hellfire and damnation. Now it is hardly acceptable to say that anyone is a 'sinner'. Do you ever regard yourself as primarily a 'sinner'? Yet each one of us is confronted at some time or another by the enormity of the harm we have done, the way we have messed up our own lives or the lives of others. Then we agree with Julian that 'sin is the sharpest scourge'.

Whatever name you give to it,
however you regard it,
sin is the sharpest scourge
with which any soul can be struck,
and every soul is struck.

We can call it our shortcomings,
failings or natural inclinations:
it still strikes at our deepest point,
binds us and blinds us
and turns us away from God,

till, walking like a blinded captive
in the victory parade of evil,
we feel there is no escape.
But while we inevitably sin,
God has acted in his power and love.

Based on Chapter 39

Julian was given this insight:

> God reminded me that I would sin, and because of the
> delight I had in contemplating him, I did not at that time take
> any notice of that showing. And our Lord very mercifully
> waited and gave me the grace to pay attention, and I applied
> the showing particularly to myself, but when I saw all the
> gracious comfort that followed, as you will see, I was taught
> that it applied not to anyone in particular, but to all my fel-
> low Christians in general.

Chapter 37

When Julian became anxious about this, she heard the Lord
assuring her that he would keep her safe:

> This word was said with more love and assurance of protec-
> tion for my soul than I can or may tell. For just as it was first

revealed to me that I would sin, so was comfort revealed –
assurance of protection for all my fellow Christians.

Chapter 37

God never stops calling us:
I love you;
attend to me;
you need me;
I am enough for you.

I can act in your life
to set you free,
to give you back your sight,
your life,
your joy.

Based on Chapter 36

Julian, in spite of seeing that everyone sins, does not regard
people as being depraved: she maintains that 'in every soul that
will be saved there is a godly will that never assents to sin and
never will' (Chapter 37).

Again and again she notes the way we constantly have to wrestle with that part of ourselves that fails to do or be the right thing,
that goes against the 'godly will' that is deep inside each one of
us. She follows the classical steps in dealing with our sins. Once
we are aware of how much we have sinned, and wish to change,
we need to turn to God and accept his love and forgiveness. 'By
contrition we are made clean, by compassion we are made ready
and by true longing for God we are made worthy' (Colledge &
Walsh, Chapter 39, page 245).

Christ is love in word and deed;
constant and wise and true.
He wishes us to be like him,
in all we are and do.

And when we fail to act in love,
as we are sure to do,
he never ceases loving us
so we should follow through,

And not despise ourselves
for failing yet again,
but hate the sin and love the soul,
in God's enduring strength.

Based on Chapter 40

A Prayer

Dear Lord, forgive me for the sins that are very obvious to
me, and help me to see those hidden areas in me that need
to change. And in seeing, may I turn to you and be forgiven.
Help me to change my outlook and lifestyle where change is
needed in order to grow in love of you and others. But when
I do fail again, which I inevitably will, help me not to despair
and turn from you but to keep on trusting in your love and
mercy. Amen.

Meditation 19

Love for Others

For God so loved the world that he gave his only Son, so that everyone who believes in him may not perish but may have eternal life.

John 3.16

You have heard that it was said, 'You shall love your neighbour and hate your enemy.' But I say to you, Love your enemies and pray for those who persecute you, so that you may be children of your Father in heaven; for he makes his sun rise on the evil and on the good, and sends rain on the righteous and on the unrighteous.

Matthew 5.43–45

Julian's life in many respects was very different from ours; her times, her society and her calling to be an anchoress, a solitary, shut up in her cell. Although some of us may live alone, we don't cut ourselves off from interacting with others on a daily basis, although, as far as we know, Julian was still part of the community. Her cell was attached to the Church of St Julian in Norwich: she had a window into the church and so was part of its worship life. We know from wills that named her as beneficiary (showing that she had friends), that she also had a maidservant. We also know that she had a window onto a public footpath so that people could come to her for spiritual guidance. One of those who did so, Margery Kempe, left a record of just such an encounter (Jantzen,

page 29). So her relationship with others may not be entirely different from ours after all. How we, as Christians, relate to others, is a
telling pointer to our relationship with God. Julian wrote down her
showings and her reflections on them for 'her fellow Christians':

> I am in the unity of love with all my fellow Christians. For it is
> in this unity of love that the life consists of all men who will be
> saved. For God is everything that is good, and God has made
> everything that is made and God loves everything that he has
> made, and if any man or woman withdraws his love from any
> of his fellow Christians, he does not love at all, because he has
> not love towards all . . . and anyone who has general love for
> his fellow Christians has love towards everything which is . . .
> And thus will I love, and thus do I love . . .
> *Colledge & Walsh, The Short Text, Chapter vi, page 134*

Does Julian only include a select number of people, just her 'fellow
Christians' and 'all men who will be saved'? What about those
who were not Christians? At that time in England almost everyone
had been baptized, and so for Julian there was virtually no one
who was 'not a Christian'. She is actually including everyone.

> For in mankind which will be saved is comprehended all, that
> is, all that is made and the maker of all; for God is in man, and
> so in man is all. And he who thus generally loves all his fellow
> Christians thus loves all, and he who loves thus is safe.
> *Colledge & Walsh, The Short Text, Chapter vi, page 134*

She also thought about those who are obviously evil, but this is
what she has been taught and not what she is shown by God:

I understand that every creature who is of the devil's condition in this life and so dies is no more mentioned before God and all his saints than is the devil, notwithstanding that they belong to the human race, whether they have been baptized or not.

Colledge & Walsh, Chapter 33, page 234

After being reminded that she and all her fellow Christians would go on sinning, and being assured of God's continuing love, she concludes:

God loves us – as we are,
with all our self-love,
all our posturing,
all our disregard for others.
As a mother does a child,
he enfolds us in his love –
fills us with his love,
turns us around and, gently
pushing us outward, says,
'Love one another,
as I love them – all of them
as if they were one soul,
all your fellow Christians,
all who will be saved,
all of humankind.'

This is not easy:
Some I ignore,
some annoy me,
others I condemn in anger,
and a few I love,
but woefully few,

though the intention is there –
to love all of humankind.

Based on Chapters 37, 38, 40

A Prayer

Lord, forgive my self-absorption, and my attempts to cover it with apparent words of concern – such hollow words.

Fill me more and more with your love, so that it flows out to others, all my fellow Christians, and beyond, to all those who sin.

As you do not withdraw your love from me, a sinner, may I hate sin, as you hate it, but endlessly love the sinner, as you love them. May I see you in every person, and so find fullness of joy. Amen

Meditation 20

What is Prayer?

Pray without ceasing, give thanks in all circumstances; for this is the will of God in Christ Jesus for you.

1 Thessalonians 5.17–18

Do you struggle to pray? Do you feel that you ought to pray and pray regularly, but your life is so busy that there is no time left for it? Or do you make time to pray but feel it is accomplishing nothing, even though there may be times when it feels as though you are being heard, and others when your prayers are answered. So you keep doggedly at it. How common these experiences are to us all. Julian was no exception, but God gave her new insights into prayer. She was first shown two important conditions on which true prayer rests:

> First, it should be the right kind of prayer (rightful prayer), namely that we do not pray for anything at all except for the thing that is God's will and to his glory; second, we should then confidently trust in the outcome.
>
> *Chapter 41*

She continues:

> And yet frequently our trust is not complete, for we are not certain that God hears us, because we wonder why he should and because we feel absolutely nothing. We are usually as barren

and dry after praying as we were before. And it is here in our feeling, our foolishness, that our weakness lies (for I have experienced this myself). I heard in my mind our Lord saying to me: 'I am the ground (foundation) of your praying. First it is my will that you have something, and then I make you desire it, and afterwards I cause you to pray for it: how then could it be that you would not get what you asked for?' I found this and what followed very encouraging.

Chapter 41

Her understanding is that prayer begins with God giving us the desire. It continues as we give ourselves more and more to God and it ends in our being more united with God. Her phrase is 'being one-d' with God. Making special requests and then waiting to see if God answers is not her definition of worthy prayer. She explains: 'Prayer is a true, gracious, lasting intention of the soul united (one-d) and bound to the will of our Lord by the inner working of the Holy Spirit' (Chapter 41).

Her advice is that we should continue to pray wholeheartedly, even though it is a struggle and seems pointless. Its very barrenness and feebleness pleases God. He accepts our good intention and hard work, no matter how we feel. So we need to persevere. On the other hand, 'We should not overdo things in our zeal: act reasonably with good sense, keeping our strength for him until we have the one we seek in fullness of joy, that is, Jesus' (Chapter 41).

This is good homely advice. Keep at it. Don't rely on feelings. Something is happening even if you are not aware of it at the time. And don't get carried away and overdo things. At the same time, she is moving us from the mundane into a more profound understanding and experience of what prayer is.

Pray as you breathe:
  when breath ceases the body dies;
    when prayer stops the soul dies.
Breathe in the Spirit,
breathe out your soul to God.

Pray as you breathe:
  with your whole heart,
    even if you feel nothing,
even if nothing seems to happen;
for if prayer stops the spirit dies.

Pray as you breathe;
  pray through the dryness and the emptiness,
    the feebleness and the malaise:
God will rejoice in you,
and hold you and lift you up.

Pray as you breathe:
  inhale oxygen, exhale carbon dioxide.
    Inhale the fresh, exhale the stale,
      breathe in the Spirit, breathe out self:
so God turns all our living into prayer.

                Based on Chapter 41

She also advises:

If you have come to God with your request;
  asked him again and again;
    implored him over and over,
but still have not received
  what you asked for,

don't be discouraged;
    don't give up.
Keep on waiting
    for a better time,
        or for more grace,
            or for a better gift.
For God has heard you,
and has your request on his heart.

Based on Chapter 42

A Prayer

I pray.
I want an answer, Lord.
I want to change the world.
I pray.
I get an answer.
All I'm going to change is you.
I pray.
Lord, change me.

Based on Chapter 43

Meditation 21

Truth, Wisdom, Love

For the Lord *gives wisdom; from his mouth come knowledge and understanding.*

Proverbs 2.6

Then God said, 'Let us make humankind in our image, according to our likeness; and let them have dominion over the fish of the sea, and over the birds of the air, and over the cattle, and over all the wild animals of the earth, and over every creeping thing that creeps upon the earth.' So God created humankind in his image, in the image of God he created them; male and female he created them.

Genesis 1.26–27

Do you regard yourself and others as basically good or basically bad? Are we sinful by nature from birth, 'born guilty, a sinner when my mother conceived me' (Psalm 51.5) or does each one have a 'God-image' within them (Genesis 1.27), which makes us all 'children of God' (1 John 3.1)? The Christian Church has been ambivalent and has swung from one view to the other at different times.

As we have seen, Julian regarded each person as basically good. She came to see them, her fellow Christians, as having something of God in them. 'For in everyone who will be saved there is a godly will that never says yes to sin and never will' (Chapter

37). 'God often showed in all the revelations that humankind is constantly doing his will to his glory' (Chapter 44).

Do you agree with Julian? Or do you find her words difficult to accept, especially seeing we are confronted daily with the hurt and violence that people do to each other? Godly will? Humankind always doing God's will? Where was Julian living? Was she, in her cell, so cut off from the world that she had lost touch with reality? What of ourselves? Can we see clearly that image of God in us or is it hidden behind a thick fog?

In the East a thick band of cloud,
foaming up from below the horizon,
monotone grey, damping down all colour,
the day's inevitable light slowly increasing,
white and unremarkable.

This is me, God's image in me,
yearning, striving to dawn,
obscured behind the dark clouds
of my ego, but there,
oh surely there.
And day's dawn says,
see, light will come;
it may be dulled down,
but it will come.

And, as I watch,
the clouds are rimmed
with a shining silver light;
transformed by the sun,
still hidden, but surely there.

Based on Chapters 44, 47

Julian wants us not to forget that we are made in God's image and we all carry that image within us. 'God is never-ending unsurpassed truth, wisdom and love, all uncreated; a person's soul has the same properties but created by God. And it always does what it was created for; it sees God, it contemplates God and it loves God' (Chapter 44).

Here again Julian sees God as triune. The Father is truth, the Son wisdom and the Holy Spirit is love, which comes from truth and wisdom.

In the light of truth we perceive God.
With the insight of wisdom we are engrossed in him,
    to our great delight,
        and this is love.

The truth and wisdom and love all come from God,
all uncreated,
    without beginning,
        without end.

But we are creatures,
created by God,
    who has set within our souls
        truth, wisdom and love.

God rejoices in us
    and we in him,
        marvelling at our maker.

But he is so exalted,
great and good
    that we come to seem
        as nothing in our own eyes,

Except that the brightness and the clarity
of truth and wisdom
keep on assuring us we are
always protected
   because we are
     made in, of and for love.

Based on Chapter 44

Julian knows how we as Christians judge one another, sometimes harshly, and now she is shown how God does not judge like that. He judges her and her fellow Christians in love, not assigning any blame. Can we do the same to ourselves and then to others?

A Prayer

Lord, help me to see myself in the light of truth,
and help me not to despair if I am appalled at what I see,
but keep on assuring me that you do not reject me or
blame me.
Give me the wisdom to trust in your willingness to forgive,
and to see the way forward.
Fill me with your love and grace
so that I can turn my failings into joy.
Lord, help me not to be judgemental towards others,
but to see your image in each one,
and to see it in love.
Amen.

Meditation 22

No Wrath in God

I am one who has seen affliction under the rod of God's wrath. The thought of my affliction and my homelessness is worm-wood and gall! My soul continually thinks of it and is bowed down within me.
But this I call to mind, and therefore I have hope: The steadfast love of the LORD never ceases, his mercies never come to an end; they are new every morning; great is your faithfulness.
Lamentations 3.1, 19–23

Anger is a basic human emotion – a reaction to the feeling that we are being treated unjustly or unkindly. Some of us react like a gun-shot going off; others allow anger to smoulder, waiting for a more considered, perhaps more devastating response. Traditionally we were taught that this is how God reacts to human wickedness.

From the Bible we learn about the anger or wrath of God: how it is kindled by evil deeds, even though God is slow to anger and holds back his wrath; how he has vented it on occasion, but mostly defers it till the Day of Judgement. As sinners we deserve God's anger and condemnation. Julian was taught the same:

And the depth of our gracious Lord's friendship is shown as he protects us while we are still sinners. More than that, he shows us our sins, to each alone, in the light of his mercy and grace. But when we see how rotten we are, we believe that God must surely be angry with us.

Chapter 40

No Wrath in God

Julian reminds us how we judge others and then think that God's judgement is the same as ours. But she was shown something quite different about God's judgement. When I look at the way I judge others, I can say:

I'm good at passing judgement,
quickly, easily, without endless
time wasted in researching facts –
sometimes leniently, but mostly
harshly and in anger, as is deserved.

Just so God, who demands perfection,
is the Great Judge,
condemning us sinners in his wrath
as we well deserve.
We all know this – the Bible tells us.

No, not so, says Julian.
We do, indeed, deserve all this –
pain, blame and wrath,
but she saw, in truth, that God
is never angry – and never will be.

He is all goodness,
all wisdom and all love.
So God would not be God
if he were angry.
Between God and our souls
there is no barrier –
only a oneness in love,
solely through his goodness.

Based on Chapter 46

If we think of how we react to being treated badly by those we love the most, don't we react more in sorrow and pain than in anger? So why would God react in anger? Even to the most appalling perpetrators of evil? For don't we believe that he loves everyone in equal measure?

When anger comes in passion raw
it can be nursed into increase
to vent itself in hurtful deed,
eye for eye or tooth for tooth.

Or else it can be buried deep
and built up, bitter layer by layer,
fermenting, churning, turning sour –
a poison loosed into the soul.

But isn't anger mostly brief?
The first defence against an act
that opens us to floods of pain,
and leaves us all alone and hurt.

'I saw no kind of wrath in God,
not for a short time nor for long.'
Most Christian folk would disagree.
'It's in the Bible', they would say.

God must be angry when he sees
the evil that the wicked do.
A vengeful God? Or one who holds
a festering anger deep inside?

I see a grieving God, a God
of grace who feels the pain, when we

reject him, scorn him, turn our backs,
destroy each other, kill the world.

We close our eyes, we will not see,
the anger is in us, not God.
He acts in mercy and forgives,
to end our anger and not his.

Based on Chapter 46

This leaves us with a dilemma. How do we reconcile the words in the Bible and the teaching of the Church with Julian's view that there is no wrath in God? It was a dilemma that Julian tried to resolve and could not, so for the time being she embraced both views, while 'waiting upon God in this matter' (Chapter 46).

A Prayer

Come to God as a gracious friend and be honest in expressing your feelings.
If it be that you feel he must be angry with you because of your failings;
if it be that you are denying some faults and need to see yourself more clearly;
if it be that you cannot accept that God is without anger and you hope in fact that he is very angry with all the perpetrators of evil;
if it be that you are an angry person and can't or won't deal with it,
express your feelings honestly and 'wait upon our Lord's will in this matter'.

Meditation 23

Being Made Meek and Mild

Blessed are the meek, for they will inherit the earth.

Matthew 5.5

We have a vision of how we should live as Christians that we try to live out day by day. But that if you are like me, day by day we fail. We are left feeling disappointed, even angry with ourselves, and sometimes decidedly desolate. We have no inner peace. Again we find that Julian has been there before us.

She reminds us that the Holy Spirit is within us, protects us and gives us back our peace, through mercy and grace. She goes on to explain how she sees mercy and grace, the two fundamental properties of God, working in our lives.

Mercy is a sweet, gracious way of working through love. Mingled with generous sympathy (plentiful pity), mercy works to protect us and mercy works to turn everything to good for us. Mercy out of love allows us to fail in some measure, and as far as we fail, so far we fall, and as far as we fall, so much we die. For we must necessarily die in the measure we fail in order to see and feel God, who is our life. Our failing is dreadful, our falling is shameful, and our dying is sorrowful. Yet in all this the sweet eye of sympathy (pity) never turns away from us, and the action of mercy never stops.

Chapter 48

We cannot escape from our human frailty; 'dying to self' is an ongoing process. We can only look back in time and see that we have become changed persons, to the extent that we have allowed God's grace and mercy to work in our lives. At the beginning I said that we have a vision of how we should live as Christians; what attributes we should embody. Some of these change over time, so that what appealed to former generations no longer appeals to us. Julian continues:

> God is our true peace. He is our sure protector when our peace has vanished, and he is constantly working to bring us back to a peace that will last. So when, by the action of mercy and grace, we are made meek and mild, then we are truly safe.
>
> *Chapter 49*

Being made 'meek and mild'?
Who would want to be meek and mild today?
When meekness equals weakness
and mildness is too wishy-washy.
Today the word is 'self-assertive';
'strive with passion' for
'you deserve the best'.
Still the old lie and the old liar
leading us further into
discord, violence, chaos.

Can you not hear your name being called?
Sin has made you deaf.
Can you not see where you are headed?
Sin has made you blind.
We are all full of anger and accusations,

lost and afraid,
falling into a vortex of black nothingness –
dreading to face an angry God.

'Look', says Julian, 'and listen.'
'I saw no anger in God of any kind –
not for long
or even for a brief moment.'

God is all love and goodness.
How could he go against his nature
and be angry?
Rather, he pours out on us
his grace and mercy,
reversing our direction –
from death to joyous life,
from shameful falling to honourable rising,
from paralysing fear to true peace.
Walking away from death and sin and fear —
Oh yes!

But towards being made meek?
No thanks! If meek is being a doormat,
being trodden on by others,
and allowing myself to be used.
But if meek is
being truly accepting of who I am,
being open to learn,
to bear Christ's yoke,
and follow where he leads,
may I be made meek.

Towards being made mild?
No thanks! If mild is being lukewarm,

insipid and neither this nor that.
But if mild is
not swinging to extremes,
not being a slave to my passions,
not being easily riled by others,
but still being passionate for the right things,
may I be made mild.

Based on Chapters 47, 48

A Prayer

What troubles you most at this point on your Christian journey? What do you strive for? What vision do you have of a
true Christian? Bring it all before our good Lord, and ask
for eyes to see both yourself and his mercy and grace in new
light and with renewed strength.

Meditation 24

The Lord and the Servant

Therefore just as one man's trespass led to condemnation for all, so one man's act of righteousness leads to justification and life for all. For just as by the one man's disobedience the many were made sinners, so by the one man's obedience the many will be made righteous. But law came in, with the result that the trespass multiplied; but where sin increased, grace abounded all the more, so that, just as sin exercised dominion in death, so grace might also exercise dominion through justification leading to eternal life through Jesus Christ our Lord.

Romans 5.18–21

Stories are often the most engaging and successful way of opening people's eyes, so that they can see a different aspect of life: Jesus used parables, the Greeks myths and Aesop fables. Julian is now shown a story, an 'example' she calls it, to answer her questions. The story comes replete with a great lord and his servant, with whom anyone contemporary with Julian would happily engage, although it may make some of us today feel uncomfortable. Nevertheless, it still has much to say to us.

Julian was troubled by contrary views – on the one hand, the teaching backed by the Bible and the Church that sin elicits blame and, on the other, her vision of a God who blames us as little as if we were pure and holy angels. She wanted to know which is true or, if both, how they hold together, since it affected her daily choices between good and evil (Chapter 50).

God answered her in an 'example' that played itself out before her eyes:

Julian watched a drama unfold before her eyes:
each detail, each action
left its imprint in her heart,
replaying over and over before her,
as for twenty years and more
she tried to fathom the depths of its meaning.

A lord, grand and kindly, sat in state,
but in a barren place.
His servant stood before him,
slightly to the left,
all attention, waiting to receive instructions.
He was dressed in a stained and worn tunic,
strangely so for the servant of a great lord.
At the lord's word,
he rushed off eager to do his bidding;
rushed off, so intent on his task,
that he fell into a deep ditch,
and lay there, injured,
helpless and devastated
at his failure.

The ditch was so narrow
that he could not see out of it;
so deep that he could not climb out.
No one was there to help,
except his lord, who was very close,
who looked at him with pity, not with blame,
who offered comfort.
But the servant could not see this.

He was too taken up with feeling desolate.
He could not lift himself out.
He was totally alone.

What did this drama, this story, this parable, mean?
At one level the meaning was clear.
The gracious and stately lord is God.
The servant is Adam,
each and every one of us
who intend to do God's will.
But time and again, we fail.
Then we thrash around,
blaming ourselves and others,
sure that God blames us too –
trying to pull ourselves up out of the ditch.

Julian saw that we are so blinded in this life
that we cannot see how close God is,
or how he commends us for our will to serve
and does not blame us for our failures.
She also saw in this drama
God's plan to remedy the situation.

This is the second and deeper meaning.
The lord is still God.
But the servant is his son, Jesus,
who 'fell' to earth
in the womb of the maiden.
The stained tunic of the servant
symbolizes Christ putting on full humanity.
The servant eagerly rushed to do the Lord's will,
just so Christ eagerly accepted his task.

As the servant fell into the deep ditch,
so Christ 'fell into' suffering on the cross.
As the servant felt all alone,
so Christ felt all alone and forsaken.
Through his willingness to fall
into suffering and abandonment,
Christ lifted us up out of our pit of guilt and sin.

Julian also came to see a deeper meaning still.
The servant is both Adam and Christ;
and we are both Adam and Christ.
The blindness and weakness we have is from Adam;
the strength and goodness from Christ.
So Christ has taken on himself all our guilt,
and God does not assign more blame to us
than to his own son.

Julian saw the end of the drama.
The servant, now dressed in sparkling clothes,
is seated on the right hand of the lord:
his crowning glory being humankind redeemed.

Based on Chapter 51

What does it mean? Julian, as we read, found it so enigmatic that it took her twenty years of meditating and wrestling with its meaning before she felt she had come to some understanding. We shall follow some of her conclusions in the rest of the book. At one level it resonates with our own experience. Can you see yourself as the servant, eager to rush off and do God's will, but soon falling into a ditch? If you get lost trying to see meanings at deeper levels, don't give up. It may take time to see more in the parable. (My deeper insight also came after mulling over its meaning for more than twenty years.)

A Prayer

Think of that part of the story you find most helpful. Start there and ask God for deeper insight and new understandings.

Meditation 25

Christ the Gardener

*When she had said this, she turned around and saw Jesus
standing there, but she did not know that it was Jesus. Jesus
said to her, 'Woman, why are you weeping? For whom are
you looking?' Supposing him to be the gardener, she said to
him, 'Sir, if you have carried him away, tell me where you
have laid him, and I will take him away.' Jesus said to her,
'Mary!' She turned and said to him in Hebrew, 'Rabbouni!'
(which means Teacher).*

John 20.14–16

What is your image of a gardener? Do you picture a lady in sunhat
with a basket over her arm and pruners in her hand dead-heading
the roses, or a man in old clothes wielding a large fork, intent on the
back-breaking task of turning over the soil in the vegetable garden?
This is more like the image that Julian had, together probably with
that of Adam and Eve being told that they will only eat bread by the
sweat of their brow. She may also have had in mind Mary Magdalene mistaking Jesus for the gardener. In the middle of the parable of
the Lord and the Servant she writes:

I wondered what sort of task the servant was given to do. Then
I saw he was to do the greatest labour and the hardest task
there is. He was to be a gardener, digging and ditching and
sweating and turning the soil over and over: to dig deep down
and to water the plants when they needed it. He was to keep
at this task, making channels for the water and producing a

bumper crop of fruit to present to the Lord. He was not to
return until he had produced all this food, to his Lord's liking.

Chapter 51

In trying to express the almost inexpressible, Julian employs
a mixture of images and concepts from her own period and
culture: first the Lord and servant and now the gardener. This
image is still familiar to us: hard work, perseverance, enabling
natural growth, producing fruit for which God waits. She
mixes her metaphors, also describing Christ digging to find a
treasure, which is both the food and us. I have expressed it like
this:

God made the earth we live on,
skies, seas, lands, creatures
and plants of every kind.
Lastly, he made us humans.
He gave us a garden for a home,
which, through our disobedience,
we threw away.

Or, let us rather say, that God
is still creating universes,
and our own small sphere:
skies, seas, lands, all life,
and humans as part of that,
all sharing a single building thread,
the coil of DNA.

Our ancestors,
Adam of the earth and
Eve, the living one, were gardeners
who worked the soil.

Christit the Gardener

Digging deep, they planted,
watered, pruned and waited –
befriended some animals and
worked with them to ensure
a plentiful supply of food.

Yet they longed to –
as we still long to, strive to –
ascend beyond the earth-aspect –
sensing the touch of God's breath,
his spirit, drawing us up into
that something beyond.

And God, at the right time,
sent his son, the second Adam,
to our earth to be a gardener.
He was to dig deep down,
turning the soil over and over,
digging, ditching and sweating,
scattering the seeds,
waiting and watching to see them sprout,
watering and weeding when necessary.

He was to persevere in his work
until the earth produced
fine, abundant fruit.
Then he was to present this
before his father:
the treasure of the earth that his father
loved and longed for –
and so make a way for us to ascend
beyond the bounds of this earth,
beyond our frailties and limitations,
to become god-like

and at the same time
fully human.

Based on Chapter 51
(from the Lord and the Servant)

The story of the Creation and Fall in Genesis is an allegory to explain our origins and sinfulness. Now that we also have a scientific explanation of the origins of our universe, our solar system and all living matter, one of the problems we wrestle with is how to hold the two together. Julian probably understood the story of Adam and Eve as an allegory and not literally true, and she used the medieval method of interpreting allegory to find spiritual truths in it, as she did in her parables. We need to use the methods of our day to find truth and meaning in these stories. So let us engage with them, puzzle over them and ask God to bring out the meaning we need now in our lives.

A Prayer

Lord, open my eyes that I may see new truths in these stories, and in myself, and enable me to live out those truths, and when I fail to do so, give me the perseverance to keep on trying. Amen.

Meditation 26

In Well and in Woe

For we know that the law is spiritual; but I am of the flesh, sold into slavery under sin. I do not understand my own actions. For I do not do what I want, but I do the very thing I hate. Now if I do what I do not want, I agree that the law is good. But in fact it is no longer I that do it, but sin that dwells within me. For I know that nothing good dwells within me, that is, in my flesh. I can will what is right, but I cannot do it. For I do not do the good I want, but the evil I do not want is what I do. Now if I do what I do not want, it is no longer I that do it, but sin that dwells within me.

Romans 7.14–20

Even if we understand the mysteries of the Trinity and of our salvation, and even if we know what God's will is, does that mean we can now live in that light? Don't we also experience with Julian that 'During our lifetime here we have in us a marvellous mixture of both well-being and woe. We have in us our risen Lord Jesus Christ, and we have in us the wretchedness and the harm of Adam's falling' (Colledge & Walsh, Chapter 52, page 279).

She goes on to say that in our dying, Christ raises us up, but our sins and pains make us so dark and blind that we find it hard to accept any comfort. We really do intend to wait for God and to trust in him – this is from his working in us as he gives us sight and new understanding in various degrees. So that at one time we are raised to well-being, but then we are allowed to fall into woe.

But if Adam's falling has infected us all with sin, and this comes naturally, and if we believe Christ's death has dealt with sin for all of us, why do we go on living in this muddle of well and woe? Why does living perfectly good lives not come naturally to us now? It may be because:

I live in a between time:
　　between the promise and its fulfilment;
　　　　between the victory and the mopping-up operations;
　　　　between the election and the inauguration.

I live in a between space:
　　between earth and air and water;
　　　　between earth and heaven;
　　　　between creation groaning in labour pains
　　　　　　and creation reborn.

I live in a between mode:
　　between wretchedness and glory;
　　　　between dark sin and bright goodness;
　　　　between blindness and vision,
　　　　　falling and rising, woe and well,
　　　　　　wandering aimlessly and pressing ahead.

And as I live in between,
　　my yearning is for God,
　　　　my intention is to wait for him,
　　　　　for he opens the eye of my understanding.

 And when I fail
　　and fall again into blindness,
　　　I will cling to him,
　　　　trusting in him to carry me –
in between.

Based on Chapter 52

So what is Julian's solution? In summarizing her conclusions, she says:

> And so all the days of our lives are lived out in this incredible muddle, but in it all God wants us to trust that he is always with us . . .
>
> In the midst of this muddle we have reason to mourn – because our sin causes Christ pain; and reason to rejoice – because he suffered as a result of love . . .
>
> While we live we will never be free of sin, but if we know and see the working of grace in our lives, we will hate nothing but sin and strive to be as free of it as possible. So when we fall – through our blindness and selfishness – let us quickly respond to God's touch of grace, and get up again, make what amends we can, and go on our way with God in love. When we are down, let us not fall into despair, and when we are up, let us not live carelessly. Let us realistically assess our weaknesses and humbly accept that but for the protection of grace we could not stand on our own even for the twinkling of an eye. So let us cling to God and trust only in him.
>
> *Chapter 52*

A Prayer

O Lord,
Between the intention and the execution
    lies a chasm deep and wide.
The one dazzles with its promises,
    the other dashes self-image to shards,
    plunging me into the depths.

My will aims at the good,
    my doing misses the mark.

Meditation 26

I long to be at one with you,
    I feel only the misery of my failures.

At one time a chink of light,
    a voice, a hope – I am with you –
I see the way ahead;
    at another falling, falling into darkness.

I do intend to bend my will to you,
    love you with all my heart and soul and strength:
but I just accommodate evil with such ease,
    and once more find myself in dark despair.

Oh Christ, protect me, save me from myself,
    I know deep down that this is how things are;
    this turmoil will be with me all my days.
So hold my hand and lead me, help me see
    beyond my human weakness, that in love
and grace, you walk ahead of me —
    and I will follow after you.
Amen.

Based on Chapter 52

Meditation 27

Human Nature

Live by the Spirit, I say, and do not gratify the desires of the flesh. For what the flesh desires is opposed to the Spirit, and what the Spirit desires is opposed to the flesh; for these are opposed to each other, to prevent you from doing what you want. But if you are led by the Spirit, you are not subject to the law.

Galatians 5.16–18

If you were asked to define human nature, how would you do it? It is something we all have some ideas about, but find difficult to put into words. Throughout the ages, philosophers, poets and scientists, among others, have tried to define it. It is generally accepted today that we are part of the animal kingdom, but that we have a consciousness about ourselves and each other, and a spiritual awareness, that distinguish us from other animals.

In order to examine different aspects of ourselves, for convenience we divide our humanness into body, mind and soul or spirit. We are also all familiar with Paul's two warring parts of our human nature, the spirit and the flesh. These two aspects roughly correspond to what Julian means, in translation, by 'substance' and 'sensuality' (Colledge & Walsh, Chapter 54), or 'essence' and 'fleshliness' (Fr John-Julian, Chapter 54). Our 'substance' or 'essence' could be thought of as the core of our being. We try to keep these entities together, as a whole, and talk of 'the self', whereas Julian talks of 'the soul'.

We have seen already that Julian has an exalted view of human nature. She sees it as being 'noble' (Chapter 54) and says: 'Greatly ought we to rejoice that God dwells in our soul; and more greatly ought we to rejoice that our soul dwells in God' (Colledge & Walsh, Chapter 54, page 285). We could put it this way:

I am a creature of this world,
of the same substance as all that lives,
all sharing the mysterious double-helix building block
that spirals, unspirals, joins and separates
and manifests in countless ways –
trees, amoebas, roses, humans.

I am a creature of this world –
two feet of flesh planted solidly,
consciously responding to signals
picked up by my senses.
But more than that,
I am a creature not of this world –
my mind can hold many worlds,
my spirit soar out and beyond
or deep within.

Can I believe that God dwells in my soul –
in the essence of who I am:
moreover, that my soul dwells in God?

That God, the uncreated,
created me to be his dwelling place;
that I dwell in God's essence,
and it is his essence that makes me what I am –
that in essence it is all God?
While God is still God
and I am his creature.

Can I believe this?
Believing, becoming one –
Adam and Eve and Christ;
body and soul and mind;
all enclosed in the Triune God;
One Lord, One God.

Based on Chapter 54

Julian is well aware that in reality we struggle to live as though
God dwells in us, as though our body, mind and soul are one, as
the Trinity is one. She goes on to say that we need to know our
own soul, or self in our words. Do any of us find this easy?

Do you know yourself?
   Do you know your own soul?
It is quicker and easier for us to know God
   than to know our own soul,
for we are enfolded in God,
   and we enfold God is us.
But equally we cannot know God
   until we know our own soul.
Although we have God within us
   from our birth, to grow
and become fully ourselves,
   we need the mercy and grace
that come from Christ,
   who became fully human for us.
So yearn to know yourself,
   yearn to know Christ in yourself,
   yearn to grow more fully into him.

Based on Chapter 56

We need to know ourselves, who we are, what drives us, what our deepest desires are. We need to see where we fail the most, where we are broken and need healing. We also need to see that in essence we are one with God, although it certainly does not seem so. And we need to acknowledge that 'We cannot be saved merely on the basis of having our natural origin in God, unless this is augmented by his mercy and grace' (Chapter 57).

A Prayer

Lord, there are some days when I feel I am making progress; when I know you have been with me, enabling me to forget myself and act out of love. Thank you for that.

So often, though, my old self comes to the fore and I know I have failed you and myself yet again. I am left feeling depressed and discouraged. I do yearn to know Christ in me. I do yearn to grow more fully into Christ. Please fill me with your Spirit so that I may do so. Amen.

Meditation 28

Substance and Sensuality

For those who live according to the flesh set their minds on the things of the flesh, but those who live according to the Spirit set their minds on the things of the Spirit. To set the mind on the flesh is death, but to set the mind on the Spirit is life and peace. For this reason the mind that is set on the flesh is hostile to God; it does not submit to God's law – indeed it cannot, and those who are in the flesh cannot please God.

But you are not in the flesh; you are in the Spirit, since the Spirit of God dwells in you.

Romans 8.5–9a

We have looked at the way in which Julian understands human nature, how we need to know ourselves and how this is linked to knowing God. Julian returns to her revelations and is able to see more meaning in them as God gives her more insight. In the previous meditation we were introduced to two aspects of human nature, as she described it: our 'substance' and 'sensuality' (Colledge & Walsh) or our 'essence' and 'fleshliness' (Fr John-Julian). We will now explore further what she meant:

> With regard to our substance (essence), he made us so noble and so rich that we are constantly doing his will to his glory. By 'we' I mean those who will be saved . . . And from this great richness and this high nobility, fitting strengths come into our soul when it is joined to our body, and in this joining we are made sensual (fleshly).
>
> *Chapter 57*

Wait a minute! We are constantly doing God's will? That's news to me. I for one know this is not true of me. How can Julian say this? She adds, however, 'And so we are complete in our substance and in our sensuality we fall short, and this shortfall God will make up by the operation of mercy and grace' (Chapter 57).

Maybe we can explain it like this:

I understand that I am and I become
a unique person,
with a body of flesh and bones and blood;
a mind – a consciousness of who I am
in relation to the world outside myself;
and a soul – an awareness of something,
some power, some existence
beyond this place, this time,
and that these different aspects
are often at odds.

Julian understood
that we are twofold by God's creating,
substantial and sensual,
our substance being our essential nature,
the substance of Being itself.
It is the higher part.

Our sensuality is us
responding through our senses,
in our minds and bodies,
in our fleshliness, to the world,
each in our own unique way.
It is the lower part.

Both belong to our soul.
The journey of faith is to unite
the two into one in our Lord,
to become fully ourselves.

Based on Chapter 58

Julian actually says that 'in Christ our two natures are united'
(Chapter 58). But we do not recognize this, nor do we easily feel
that it has already happened. Sin gets in the way.

Iniquities, sins, trespasses, failings –
whatever we call it,
we do not act as we should;
we do not think as we should.
Our hearts, our wills, our intentions
are daily engaged in battle:
the battle between
our true selves – what we want to be;
and our actual selves – what, alas, we are.

But, says Julian, see that truly it belongs
to our human nature to hate sin;
and as much as sin is ugly and unclean
it is also unnatural.
But sin is inevitable;
it is necessary for us to fall –
and it is necessary for us to see it,
and to turn to our Mother Jesus,
whose love never falters or diminishes.

A child does not by nature rely on itself,
a child does not by nature disregard its mother,
but relies on her strength.

It is natural for a child to love its mother,
and for the mother to return that love.
For we recognize in this life no state
more powerless and dependent
than the state of childhood.

As we have our natural being in our Father God,
we return into him through the grace of our Mother Jesus.
Then we shall know the meaning of the words,
'All shall be well,
    and you will see for yourself
        that every kind of thing shall be well.'

Based on Chapter 63

Julian's image of Jesus as a mother may seem very innovative and strange to you. We will think more about this in the next meditation.

A Prayer

Lord, I wish I could claim that I always do your will, but I don't. I want to and sometimes I try, but on the whole I do what my will dictates. Help me to be like a child again and to follow your lead as a child follows a mother. May I learn to depend on you. Unite my warring parts, O Lord, and make me whole. Amen.

Meditation 29

Jesus our Mother

'Jerusalem, Jerusalem, the city that kills the prophets and stones those who are sent to it! How often have I desired to gather your children together as a hen gathers her brood under her wings, and you were not willing!'

Matthew 23.37

If you try to imagine God, what image comes to mind? What of Jesus? He is easier to picture because he became a person of flesh and blood, a Jew in first-century Palestine. We probably picture both as male: God as Father and Jesus as a young man of thirty or so – unsurprisingly, since this is how the Bible portrays them both. Today many of us try to move away from exclusively male images and language about God. Julian takes a leap ahead of us when she speaks of Jesus as our Mother.

And so in our creation God almighty is our loving Father, and God all wisdom is our loving Mother, with the love and the goodness of the Holy Spirit, which is all one God, one Lord . . .

In our almighty Father we have our protection and our happiness, with regard to our natural essence (substance), which is ours from without beginning; and in the second person, in knowledge and wisdom, we have our protection with regard to our fleshliness (sensuality), together with our restoration and our salvation, for he is our Mother, brother and saviour;

and in our good Lord the Holy Spirit we have our reward
and our recompense for our living and our labour . . .

Chapter 58

Julian compares Jesus to a mother carrying, giving birth to and
then nurturing a child.

Jesus, our Lord,
Jesus, our Brother,
Jesus, our Friend,
Jesus, our Saviour,
Jesus, striding ahead of his disciples,
   dark-skinned, dark-haired,
    with a dark beard,
   a compassionate expression
   and deep penetrating eyes –
that is the Jesus who emerges
   from the screen of my mind.

But Jesus as Mother?
   so much harder to envisage –
    to embrace, as Julian did.

Our mother carried us in her womb
   to full term,
   gave birth in pain,
   to a life of toil and death.
Jesus, our true Mother,
   carries us within him
   in love and travail,
   and births us in the cruellest pain
   to joy and abundant life.

Our mother nourished us at her breast.
Mother Jesus feeds us with himself,
    the precious food of true life,
    and sustains us most generously
    with the sacraments
    and the word.

We grow, we exert our independence
    we fall and get hurt –
    our mother is there to wash the wounds
    and hold us tight.
Jesus encourages us
    to grow to full humanity,
    and is always there
    to tend our wounds.

We fail and do what is wrong –
    our mother chastises us
    and teaches us what is right.
So our Lord does –
    with forgiveness and love.
He shows us the way –
    He is the Way.

And his love is always
    the nearest to us,
    the readiest to embrace us,
    and the surest there is.
He is longing for us to love him,
    as our true Mother, in return.

Based on Chapters 59, 60

Let us bring together in a prayer the ways in which Julian sees
that Jesus Christ is our Saviour, Brother and Mother.

A Prayer

Jesus Christ, my Saviour,
　　you became a human being, as I am;
　　　　you died for me,
　　　　　　but you rose from the dead
　　　　　　　　to break the power of evil.

Jesus Christ, my Brother,
　　you enabled me to become a new person,
　　　　a child of God our Father.

Jesus Christ, my Mother,
　　you carried me within you,
　　　　in love and great pain,
　　　　　　suffering to give me birth.
　　You feed me with yourself,
　　　　the precious food of true life,
　　　　　　that sustains me fully.
You know my needs and watch over me with love,
　　and protect me as I grow.
You give me freedom and independence,
　　to grow to full maturity.

So continue to enlarge my understanding;
direct my ways;
keep my conscience sharp to avoid sin;
comfort my soul when it aches;
and flood my heart with light
when it is overcome with darkness.
Give me as much knowledge as I am able to grasp,
and gracious memory of your suffering and humanity.

Help me always to be filled with wonder and thanks
  at your great goodness,
    to love what you love,
      to be well satisfied with all you have done.

When I fail you,
  when I fall into old ways,
    when sin gets the better of me,
  please bend down and
    lift me up again,
      wash me clean,
        and point me in the right direction;
Jesus, my Saviour, Brother, Mother.
Amen.

Based on Chapter 62

Meditation 30

As a Child Growing Up

Now this I affirm and insist on in the Lord: you must no
longer live as the Gentiles live, in the futility of their minds.
That is not the way you learned Christ!
For surely you have heard about him and were taught in
him, as truth is in Jesus. You were taught to put away your
former way of life, your old self, corrupt and deluded by its
lusts, and to be renewed in the spirit of your minds, and to
clothe yourselves with the new self, created according to the
likeness of God in true righteousness and holiness.

Ephesians 4.17, 20–4

We are all very familiar with the picture of the Christian life as
being 'born again' in Christ; not so familiar with the image of
Christ as our Mother. New birth does imply that we should live
as completely different persons, and this is reinforced by Paul in
his letter to the Ephesians (4.24), where he depicts us as 'new
creatures', although we are all aware that we carry the 'old creature' with us still. The picture of us as children growing up may
be more apt. A gradual change will come with growth.

Julian has a picture of Christ our Mother nurturing this growth:

By as much as our soul is more precious in his sight than our
flesh, he kindles our understanding, he prepares our way, he
eases our conscience, he comforts our soul, he enlightens our
heart, he gives us in some measure knowledge and love of
himself as the Lord, with gracious recollection of his dearest

humanity and his blessed Passion and in awesome wonder of his supreme goodness. He enables us to love all that he loves because of our love for him, and to be well satisfied with him and with all his works.

Chapter 61

An ideal picture. Again we ask why we are not like that. We seem to be doing well at one stage, but the next moment we fail, and fail miserably – so much so that we want to hide, from ourselves, from others and especially from God. We want to avoid God's presence, to give up on our spiritual practices because they don't work:

On the screen of my mind I have a picture
    of myself, all put together,
        loving and good, just as I wish.
The reality makes me cringe;
    as I say and do the wrong thing –
        yet again.

I want to run and hide, afraid to come
    into the presence of God,
        who is pure love and goodness.
But I need not fear God.

I should fear the alternatives,
        and rather come and lament
            before Jesus, my Mother.

He will wash me clean again with his blood,
    make my soul pliable and receptive
        and restore me to my true beauty,
            over the course of time.

And he will never stop doing this,
   till I and all his beloved children
      are made one with him,
         to his glory
         and our everlasting joy.

Based on Chapter 63

And so we are children who are in the process of growing up.
Growth does not happen quickly. We could use another picture
and say we have set out on a journey.

We are God's children,
by nature, birthed from him,
by grace, being brought back into him:
a second birth,
yes, but a process,
a growth, a journey.

Our journey may be full of pain;
we may feel weary and dispirited;
the Lord may seem absent;
we may long for it all to end.

Can we hear, then, with Julian,
words of comfort:
we will be taken from this pain
and come up above
to have Christ as our reward
and be filled with joy,
for he has not forgotten us.

Can we remember this
and concentrate on his promises and consolations

as fully as we can,
and accept our waiting and our distress
as lightly as we can,
counting them as nothing?

For the less we concentrate on our pains
because of our love,
the less we will feel them,
and the more they will be transformed
into thanks and honours.

Based on Chapters 64, 65

A Prayer

Where are you on your journey; in an easy-going and relaxing place or in a worrying and fearful one?

Wherever you are, picture yourself as a young child coming to share with Jesus, your mother, your joy, your sorrow or your fears. Picture his arms around you and his shared joy or his words of comfort. Concentrate on Jesus and his love and ask him to transform any pain and distress you are dealing with into thanks and honours.

Meditation 31

You Will Not Be Overcome

Who will separate us from the love of Christ? Will hardship,
or distress, or persecution, or famine, or nakedness, or peril, or
sword? As it is written, 'For your sake we are being killed all
day long; we are accounted as sheep to be slaughtered.' No, in
all these things we are more than conquerors through him who
loved us. For I am convinced that neither death, nor life, nor
angels, nor rulers, nor things present, nor things to come, nor
powers, nor height, nor depth, nor anything else in all creation,
will be able to separate us from the love of God in Christ Jesus
our Lord.

Romans 8.35–39

Julian, you will remember, received all her revelations when she was
desperately ill. When it seemed that these had come to an end, her
illness returned to such an extent that she doubted that they had
been real. Her only reality now was her physical pain. She even told
someone who came to see her that she had been raving, and then felt
an utter wretch that she had doubted so easily.

See how wretched I was! This was a great sin and a great
ingratitude, that I was so foolish, because of a little bodily pain
that I felt, as to abandon so imprudently the strength of all this
blessed revelation from our Lord God. Here you can see what I
am in myself; but our courteous Lord would not leave me so.

Colledge & Walsh, Chapter 66, page 311

Then Christ came to her again with her last showing, in which she saw that the Blessed Trinity dwells in our soul, and she heard Christ reassuring her:

> Know it well, it was no hallucination that you saw today, but accept and believe it and hold firmly to it, and comfort yourself with it and trust in it, and you will not be overcome.
>
> *Colledge & Walsh, Chapter 68, page 314*

> And these words: You will not be overcome, were said very insistently and strongly, for certainty and strength against every tribulation which may come. He did not say: You will not be troubled, you will not be belaboured, you will not be disquieted; but he said: You will not be overcome.
>
> *Colledge & Walsh, Chapter 68, page 315*

When things go horribly wrong for us, what do we do? Do we remember some of God's promises' such as 'Because you have made the LORD your refuge . . . no evil shall befall you' (Psalm 91.9–10) or 'The LORD will keep you from all evil' (Psalm 121.7)? These may now appear to be hollow. What about Paul's promise that 'all things work together for good for those who love God' (Romans 8.28)? At times this may bring some comfort, but there may be situations when you just cannot see how any good could possibly come from what has happened. This has been my experience.

> In my deep distress, O Lord,
> I turned to your promises;
> I shouted them to you;
> I flung them back at you:

'The Lord protects you',
'The Lord will deliver you',
'No evil will befall you,
for his angels will bear you up
so that you do not dash your foot
against a stone.'

I clung to these, O Lord,
but there was no protection;
no deliverance – no angels
to lift our son up – only the stones
dashing his head – the waters covering him,
death claiming him.
   What about your promises –
   O Lord, where were you?

Then I remembered those other promises;
promises that Jesus made:
   'The gate is narrow and the way hard.'
   'You have a cross to carry daily.'
   'The world will hate you.'

For he did not say,
   'You will not be tempted,
   You will not be troubled,
   You will not be distressed.'
But he did promise,
   'You will not be overcome.'

No easy ride, no special privileges;
cling only to his promise to love you:
whether things are going well,

or everything is falling apart,
  be strong in your faithful trust,
for you will not be overcome.

Based on Chapter 68

As Christ lifted Julian up again and reassured her, he repeated the words he had given her before, and she took these as being significant – to remember and hold on to.

  Six words were given to Julian;
  six words reassuring her;
  six words encapsulating the gospel:
  Accept, Believe, Hold,
  Comfort, Trust, Overcome.

  Accept what Christ has done for you.
  Believe in him with all your heart.
  Hold on to him with all your strength.
  Comfort yourself in his love.
  Trust yourself to his care
  and you will not be Overcome.

Based on Chapter 70

A Prayer

Lord, I accept all that you have done for me, in coming into our world, and in dying for me. I believe in you with all my heart, in your constant love and presence. Help me to hold on to you at all times, especially those times when I feel you have abandoned me, and to trust myself to your care, so that I find comfort in you, and go forward knowing that whatever happens I will not be overcome. Amen.

Meditation 32

Onslaught

Discipline yourselves; keep alert. Like a roaring lion your adversary the devil prowls around, looking for someone to devour. Resist him, steadfast in your faith, for you know that your brothers and sisters throughout the world are undergoing the same kinds of suffering. And after you have suffered for a little while, the God of all grace, who has called you to his eternal glory in Christ, will himself restore, support, strengthen, and establish you. To him be the power for ever and ever. Amen.

1 Peter 5.8–11

So often we find that a breakthrough moment in our faith – a time of moving forward and accomplishing something worthwhile – is followed, not by a peaceful period of joy and growth, but by sudden and inexplicable doubt. We might even feel that we are being assailed by malign forces. It is a time of testing, of temptation. Christ was baptized and heard the voice of his Father praising him, immediately after which he was sent to the desert to be tempted or assaulted by the Devil.

Having received fifteen of her visions, Julian's illness returned with increased pain and she was overwhelmed with doubt, as we have seen (Chapter 66). She fell asleep and had a nightmare in which the Fiend came to her and tried to kill her, but was unable to do so. It was so vivid that she was convinced it was real. When she woke, God showed her the last showing, in which she saw the soul as a city, with Christ sitting in the centre of it.

And the soul is wholly occupied by the blessed divinity, sovereign power, sovereign wisdom and sovereign goodness. The place which Jesus takes in our soul he will nevermore vacate, for in us is his home of homes and his everlasting dwelling . . . the blessed Trinity rejoices without end in the creation of man's soul.

Colledge & Walsh, Chapter 68, page 313

At that the Devil renewed his attack, and she was hard put to ward off despair. What did she do?

I set my eyes on the same cross in which I had seen comfort before, my tongue to speaking of Christ's Passion and repeating the faith of Holy Church, and my heart to clinging to God with all my trust and strength . . . And I despised him [the fiend], and so I was delivered from him by the strength of Christ's Passion. For it is so that the fiend is overcome, as our Lord Jesus Christ said before.

In all this blessed revelation, our good Lord gave me to understand that the vision would pass, and it is faith which preserves the blessed revelation through God's own good will and his grace.

Colledge & Walsh, Chapter 70, page 316

When she looked back she saw that, when she needed it, Christ showed himself to her in two different 'demeanours'. The word is actually 'faces', and could be translated as countenances, expressions, attitudes or demeanours, as Colledge and Walsh do. We could also say Christ showed her two aspects of himself: his compassion and his Passion. She envisaged a third – his glory.

When we are knocked to the ground by suffering or grief, left gasping and numb,

feeling we cannot go on,
Christ comes to us in the demeanour of his Passion,
showing us his face of suffering.
In our sorrow we see he has been there too:
in our pain we see his pain,
so he can carry ours.

When we are under attack by forces outside ourselves,
intentional or random,
punch-drunk with violence, tragedy, evil,
Christ is there already in the demeanour of his Passion,
but now as victor over evil,
fielding the assault, bearing the pain.

When we are brought low by our own sin,
left feeling wretched and worthless,
Christ comes to us in his demeanour of compassion,
showing us his face of sympathy, and understanding.
He can protect us from our enemy,
from doubt and despair,
and set us on our way again.

Then there is the third demeanour,
that of his radiant face of glory,
given to us in brief moments by the Spirit,
to inspire and enlighten us:
caught as a vision of what awaits us.

For now we only see, as it were,
a poor reflection in a mirror,
but then we will see face to face –
Our Risen Lord.

Based on Chapter 71

A Prayer

Lord, when I am assailed by suffering or grief, filled with despair at my own failings, or when I feel that my faith is wavering because of assault from outside, show me yourself, your Passion, your compassion, your power over all that would tear me from you, and walk beside me on the way. Amen.

Meditation 33

Seeing God More Clearly

In this you rejoice, even if now for a little while you have had to suffer various trials, so that the genuineness of your faith – being more precious than gold that, though perishable, is tested by fire – may be found to result in praise and glory and honour when Jesus Christ is revealed. Although you have not seen him, you love him; and even though you do not see him now, you believe in him and rejoice with an indescribable and glorious joy, for you are receiving the outcome of your faith, the salvation of your souls.

1 Peter 1.6–9

Julian now begins to pick up on issues and themes from earlier chapters. We could say she is summarizing her major points and emphasizing certain important aspects as she brings it all to a conclusion.

When you read about Julian being given her showings or about other Christians who have seen visions of Christ appearing to them, don't you think 'If only Jesus would come to me like that, I could also be a much more effective Christian'? Yet at times we are all given some experience of God being with us, some glimpse of the joy that being united with him brings.

Sometimes we experience –
it may be brief, but intense –
a sense of God's presence,
an epiphany,

and in the joy that we feel,
we know we have seen God.

This vanishes as quickly as it came,
as we turn our eyes away,
focusing on ourselves,
content with the less, and some days
we are plummeted into a deep darkness,
when we admit what harmful things
we have done or said.

It is done and it hurts
both the victim and the inflictor.
We feel the vast chasm
between goodness and sin,
clear sight and blindness,
heaven and hell,
bliss and anguish.
We are dead to any sight of God.
But be reassured,
we are not dead in the sight of God,
for he does not depart from us,
but waits for us
to open our eyes
and truly see him again.

Based on Chapter 72

We continue to live with contrasts, at one time seeing God in a clear light, and feeling his presence, at another seeing how we keep on giving the Devil a foothold in our life, the one resulting in the 'highest bliss', the other in the 'deepest pain' (Chapter 72).

Why are we not able to see God all the time? We know with Julian that the cause is our sin.

In this showing I saw that sin is the extreme opposite of this (of the highest bliss), and as long as we have anything to do with any sort of sin, we shall never see clearly God's blessed face. And the more dreadful and grievous our sins, the further we are at that time from seeing this blessed sight.

Chapter 72

As committed Christians we don't choose to 'have anything to do with any sort of sin'. In fact we try to avoid it, but the paradox is that the further we are along the road on our journey of faith, the more aware we are of our sins, and the more 'dreadful and grievous' they seem.

We live all the time with paradox – the two opposites exist together, the highest joy and the deepest pain, well and woe, mirth and mourning. We find daily that there is matter for mirth and matter for mourning (Chapter 72).

Our Lord God
    dwells now in us,
    is here with us,
    embraces us,
    enfolds us in his tender love,
is nearer to us
    than tongue can tell
    or heart can think,
in such a way
    that he can never leave us.
What matter for mirth,
    what cause to rejoice.

But we are earthbound,
    weighed down
    by our mortal bodies,
    groping in the dark,

our spiritual sight so blind
  that we can scarcely believe.
We long to look
  and see him clearly,
  face to face.
What matter for mourning,
  what cause to weep.

Based on Chapter 72

We may shed tears of remorse, literally or figuratively, when we realize how we have failed again to live up to our best intentions; we may feel that God must be thoroughly fed up with us, even angry, at what we have done, or failed to do – yet again. This, says Julian, is how it is while we are in this world, but she assures us that though we may feel God is far from us, he will never leave us, and we ought constantly to know this. She concludes by declaring that the purpose of all her revelations was to give us three kinds of knowledge. May God grant them to us.

A Prayer

Lord, I pray for three kinds of knowledge:
May I know you, my Lord and Saviour.
May I know myself –
who I am by nature,
and who I am becoming, through your grace.

Help me to know what my sins and my weaknesses are,
      at the same time recognizing
      that they are not me –
      that my true self is opposed to these.
Amen.

Based on Chapter 72

Meditation 34

Two Besetting Sins

Therefore, since we are surrounded by so great a cloud of witnesses, let us also lay aside every weight and the sin that clings so closely, and let us run with perseverance the race that is set before us, looking to Jesus the pioneer and perfecter of our faith, who for the sake of the joy that was set before him endured the cross, disregarding its shame, and has taken his seat at the right hand of the throne of God. Consider him who endured such hostility against himself from sinners, so that you may not grow weary or lose heart.

Hebrews 12.1–3

If you were asked to name the two sins that cause the most harm and suffering today, which would top your list? Do you think of harmful actions or the motivation behind them? Jesus was focusing our attention on what motivates sin when he said, for example, that if you are angry with anyone or insult them, you are as guilty as the murderer. Think of the two sins that trouble you the most: the two besetting sins in your life. Are they on the traditional list of seven deadly sins – wrath, greed, sloth, pride, lust, envy, gluttony – or are they something else? Julian was shown two sins, which she calls 'sickness', that plague Christians the most.

God showed two kinds of sickness that we have. One is impatience or sloth, because we bear our labour and our pain heavily. The other is despair or doubtful fear ... I am speaking of such men and women as for the love of God hate sin and dispose themselves to do God's will. Then by our spiritual blindness and bodily sluggishness we are most inclined to these; and therefore it is God's will that they should be known, and then we should reject them as we do other sins.

Colledge & Walsh, Chapter 73, page 322

Sloth and despair? The two besetting sins? They were not top of my list, so I tried to understand why Julian regarded these two as such serious sins. In the short text she names only impatience and despair, which results from doubtful fears (Short text, Chapter xxiv, page 167). Despair, also known as 'accidie', was always regarded as a sin in medieval Christianity, and I think it troubles us as much, as does impatience. But do we regard them as sins?

Seven sins beset our world,
seven named and listed,
seven we can assess ourselves against,
and tick off or cross out –
guilty or not guilty.
But for Julian two stand out above the others,
two that beset us Christians,
those whose lives are turned towards God,
who aim to do his will.

Impatience or sloth and despair?
We could call them *three* besetting sins:
impatience *and* sloth and despair.
But sins? That trouble me the most?
If I allow them a foothold –
allow them a stranglehold?

I want things to come right now;
I want myself to be put right now,
by the power of the Spirit,
without too much effort on my part.

131

It doesn't happen.
It doesn't work.
Nothing changes.
Same old world.
Same old me.

I look at the world and feel depressed,
I look at myself and I despair,
so I sit back and do nothing.

Impatience, sloth and despair,
sapping my strength,
draining my motivation,
killing my spirit,
and more than that,
stifling God's work in me.

Based on Chapter 73

So perhaps we can agree with Julian that these are serious sins for
Christians and that we should acknowledge and deal with them as
such. How do we do this? For Julian, love is the answer. We need
to keep on seeing how God loves us, how much love Christ showed
for us in his Passion, and not neglect the Holy Spirit, who for Julian
is love.

And it is about this knowledge that we are most blind, for some
of us believe that God is almighty and may do everything, and
that he is all wisdom and can do everything, but that he is all
love and wishes to do everything, there we fail.

Colledge & Walsh, Chapter 73, page 323

A Prayer

God,
I believe that you are the creator of all that is.
I believe that you are all powerful, so that
        you can do anything and everything.
I believe that you are all wisdom, so that you know what to do
and how to do anything and everything.
I believe that you are all love, so that
        you want to do anything and everything for us.
I believe – and yet I don't, I can't,
I doubt, I wonder.
Why do I struggle so?
Why is it not easier to love,
    to emerge from my laziness,
    to set aside my doubts,
    to stop being so impatient
    and to let love empower me?

Help me to believe in my very depths
that you are indeed power, wisdom and love,
and let that belief permeate
  my relationships
    my actions,
      my very life. Amen.

Based on Chapter 73

Meditation 35

Keeping the Balance

The fear of the Lord is the beginning of knowledge; fools despise wisdom and instruction.

Proverbs 1.7

There is no fear in love, but perfect love casts out fear; for fear has to do with punishment, and whoever fears has not reached perfection in love.

1 John 4.18

We use the image of walking the tightrope when we feel we are being pulled in many directions at the same time; so many choices to make, so many pitfalls to avoid as we try to keep our balance. Sometimes this leaves us paralysed with fear.

Our lives seem much more complicated than Julian's and maybe they are, but she still experienced the same fears that we do, the same ups and downs. She shifted from feeling too zealous in her faith to becoming neglectful; she found she approached God too casually and then became so fearful because of her sins that she turned away from him.

She names four spiritual fears that Christians experience. First, they are afraid of being attacked by demons. (We might not put it into these words.) Second, they fear pain and the ultimate pain of hell. Third, they have doubtful fears. But each of these, in order to escape them, can drive us into the arms of God. The fourth fear is the only positive one. It is reverent fear (Chapter 74). But what is reverent fear?

Fear is our friend to keep us safe.
Fear puts out a hand to hold us back,
saying – don't go there, don't do that –
it is dangerous, it will cause you harm.
Too little and we get hurt;
too much and we are paralysed –
so we fear the dark,
the assailant,
fire, water, malevolence,
the unknown.

We fear our inner darkness too;
our own ability to harm and
the consequences of our actions.
Too little and we could go very wrong,
too much and we are paralysed.

And the fear of God?
The great unknown,
all powerful Judge and Lord of Hosts?
Too little and we minimize
his righteousness and justice,
to our own harm;
too much and we minimize
his love and goodness
and are paralysed by despair.

But reverent fear – this pleases God:
it is our gentle friend,
our loving brother;
it leads us to run from anything not good
into our Lord's arms,
as a child runs into its mother's –
knowing how weak we are

and how much we need him –
with all our intention,
clinging to his goodness and love.

So we as God's servants and children
should hold him in reverent fear
for his Lordship and Fatherhood,
and we should love him for his goodness.

Based on Chapter 74

So we love God and we fear him. Julian goes on to say that:

> Love and fear are brothers, and they are rooted in us by
> the goodness of our Creator, and they will never be taken
> from us without end. It is our nature to love, and we are
> given grace to love; and it is our nature to fear, and we
> are given grace to fear. It is proper to God's lordship and
> his fatherhood to be feared, as it is proper to his good-
> ness to be loved . . . And yet this reverent fear and love
> are not the same, but they are different in kind and in
> effect, and neither of them may be obtained without the
> other.

Colledge & Walsh, Chapter 74, page 324

The word 'fear', as Julian uses it, seems out of place in this con-
text. We would probably today use the word 'revere' or 'hold in
awe'. In the light of this she goes on to talk of the wisest act and
the greatest foolishness. What are they?

Like a pendulum swinging
from side to side,
we swing from good to bad,

from wisdom to folly,
from joy to despair:
swinging from side to side
is life –
we needs must.

The wisest act is,
in goodness and wisdom and joy,
to attach ourselves to Christ,
to stay with him, learning his ways,
becoming what he would want.

But swing to the opposite extreme,
and entangle with wrong,
then, in this great foolishness,
we may feel we have swung right out
of the orbit of Christ's care
and into the despair
that fears to appear before him again.

The wisest act
and the greatest foolishness.

Based on Chapter 74

A Prayer

Lord, I bow before you,
    as the mighty and holy one,
    in reverent fear.

Lord, I come before you,
    as familiar a friend
    as my heart could imagine

and my soul desire,
in intimacy.

Help me to hold both the one
and the other
in perfect balance,
and as I walk the tightrope of life,
may I keep well balanced
in every way.
Amen.

Based on Chapters 74, 77

Meditation 36

Life is Penance

For this very reason, you must make every effort to sup-
port your faith with goodness, and goodness with knowl-
edge, and knowledge with self-control, and self-control
with endurance, and endurance with godliness, and godli-
ness with mutual affection, and mutual affection with love.
For if these things are yours and are increasing among you,
they keep you from being ineffective and unfruitful in the
knowledge of our Lord Jesus Christ. For anyone who lacks
these things is short-sighted and blind, and is forgetful of the
cleansing of past sins.

2 Peter 1.5–9

Julian continues to reiterate what she has been shown, at the same time giving practical counsel for daily living. She now tackles the practice of penance. The views of Julian's time were set down by the Church. Today, Christians hold widely differing views. How do you see it?

We try to live our lives as Christ would have us live, and inevitably we fail. What do we do then? Don't we try to put things right? To do something to make up for the wrong we have done? In other words, do penance? This may not be part of your church background; it was absent from mine, but the idea is still there. Let us consider whether it is helpful.

Julian has this to say when we fail and need a remedy for the malaise of sin:

The remedy is
to acknowledge our wretchedness,
and hurry back to the Lord,
for always
the sooner we admit our wrongfulness
the better it is for us.
For we know that
we deserve the pain we experience.

And we know that God has the power
to punish us fully,
and the wisdom to punish us wisely,
but never forget
that he is full of goodness and
loves us tenderly.

Based on Chapter 77

If we try to put things right ourselves, Julian has a word for us:

I was not shown specifically any penance one could take upon oneself. But I was particularly and clearly shown in a most loving manner that we should accept and take upon ourselves with meekness and patience the penance that God himself gives us, remembering his blessed passion.

Based on Chapter 77

If we are in some way castigating ourselves, she hears Christ say:

Don't think that your troubles and sorrows
are all your own fault.

Life is Penance

I don't want you to be
   unreasonably depressed.
Listen to what I tell you;
   whatever you do you will have woe.
I want you wisely to understand this
   and humbly to accept it as a kind of penance.
Then you will see that your whole life
   will actually profit from this.

For this earth is prison;
   this life is penance.
Christ wants us to rejoice in this;
   to see it and embrace it,
for he is with us,
   guarding us,
     and guiding us
       into fullness of joy.

Based on Chapter 77

'This earth is prison' and 'this life is penance' may seem a bit tough
and gloomy, even though Julian adds that we should rejoice. How
can we understand her words as being relevant for us today?

What is penance?
A way of dealing with our sin
   within the body of the Church.
When I realize how wrongly I have acted,
   I confess to a priest.
     He pronounces me forgiven
      and gives me a task to do as a penance.

So what is this penance?
   Punishment for the sin?

A way of putting things right with God?
An act to try and undo the wrong I have done?
Some way of easing my conscience?

For good or for bad penance has not been
in my vocabulary.
I am justified by faith, not by works.
It is what Christ has done for me,
not what I can do to make amends.
When I realize how wrongly I have acted,
I come before Christ to confess
and I know, by faith, I am forgiven.
And what then?
Do I go out and live as before?

No, as a new creature in Christ,
I live for him.
I walk in his way;
I have the gift of his Spirit;
I am one with him.
And I know, all the time,
how wretchedly I fail,
how much the old creature is still around.

This is Julian's penance:
to know in her heart and her mind,
with compassion, who she is,
and who in Christ she could become,
and to accept that in this life
she would never achieve it.

Nevertheless to keep on rejoicing
that Christ was with her,

guarding her
and leading us
into fullness of joy.

And for us, to live at least
  with our eyes turned
    in another direction,
  to know in our hearts and minds,
    with compassion, who we are,
      and who in Christ we could become:
our penance to act now
  towards making amends,
    towards healing wounds,
      towards giving something back,
but out of gratitude and love,
  accepting, too, our woeful inadequacy.

And, with Julian,
to keep on rejoicing
  that Christ is with us,
    guarding us
    and leading us
    into fullness of joy.

Based on Chapters 77, 81

A Prayer

Prayerfully consider how you regard the idea that life is penance. Ask for God to lead you into seeing something new for yourself in this.

Meditation 37

Consolation and Desolation

For all who are led by the Spirit of God are children of God. For you did not receive a spirit of slavery to fall back into fear, but you have received a spirit of adoption. When we cry, 'Abba! Father!' it is that very Spirit bearing witness with our spirit that we are children of God, and if children, then heirs, heirs of God and joint heirs with Christ – if, in fact, we suffer with him so that we may also be glorified with him.

Romans 8.14–17

When we have been on our Christian journey for some time we experience moments when we feel we are getting somewhere. We find consolation in the fact that we have overcome some fault or that our prayer life is more regular and meaningful. But when we are reminded of the demands that Jesus makes on us and we see how we have failed to meet them, we are sometimes plunged into desolation. Julian assures us this is to be expected and gives us some practical advice.

We remember Christ saying
we should be perfect as our
heavenly Father is perfect –
we remember it,
in the light of our own failures,

our feebleness –
we remember it and despair.

But God knows us each one
and wants us to remember four things:

Remember that he is the foundation
on which our life and being is built.

Remember that, while we are struggling
against the fierce onslaught of the enemy –
and succumbing, more often than not –
quite unawares, he protects us,
mightily and mercifully.

Remember that he gently nudges us
into awareness of how far off the path
we have strayed.

And remember that he does not turn his back on us,
but steadfastly waits for us
to turn back to him;
to set out again on the right path;
united to him in love,
as he is always to us.

Based on Chapter 78

We also need to keep in mind:

All of this friendly (familiar) showing of our gracious (courteous) Lord is a lesson of love, and a sweet gracious teaching
by him to comfort our soul. For he wants us to know by the

sweetness of his intimate (familiar) love that everything we
see or sense in opposition to this is not from him, but from
the Enemy.

Chapter 79

Jesus, our Saviour, constantly
walks with us, though
we are never constantly
aware of this –
we fail him, we fail others,
we fail ourselves,
when we fall into sin,
through our own blindness,
and weakness.

Then when we see just how wretched we are,
we want to be swallowed up
in a black hole
where we beat ourselves
over the head,
in endless self-accusation.

Jesus wants us to see our sin,
yes, and acknowledge it,
but not to get stuck there,
overflowing with our own misery.

He waits for us continually,
moaning and mourning until
we turn and pay attention to him:
and as we turn towards him
he reaches out to us,

lifts us up
and hugs us to himself.

Wretchedness and mourning
become joy and delight –
to us, to him,
to the whole company of heaven.

Based on Chapter 79

Our gracious (courteous) Lord revealed, very surely and
very powerfully, how never-ending and unchangeable is his
love, and how great his goodness and his gracious protection
of our spirit, so that the love between him and our souls will
never ever be severed.

Chapter 79

The picture of ourselves as children growing up with Jesus as our
mother is again helpful:

There is a bond between a mother and her child,
that starts when she first
holds him in her arms, a tiny helpless, wrinkled baby.
It is a bond, based on the love that flows
from the mother's heart;
on her desire, above all else,
to protect her child and see him prosper.

And if the child
takes all he can from his mother,
and heads off in the wrong direction,
heedless of the well-being of his own soul,

with never a thought for her welfare –
still, she never stops loving him,
never stops trying to protect him,
even as she stands alone with an aching heart,
sorrowing and grieving,
waiting, waiting for him to come home.

Just so is Jesus Christ that mother:
and if we are that child,
let us turn quickly and head for home,
and not leave him any longer,
standing alone,
waiting for us to come back to him.

Based on Chapter 80

A Prayer

Lord, you are a mother to me. May we laugh together as you hug me to yourself and praise me, for I need times of consolation.

But when I run away or even quietly neglect you, gently nudge me into awareness again, and if, being aware, I feel disconsolate, let me see that your arms are still outstretched waiting for me to turn back to you. Amen.

Meditation 38

Sin is a Chronic Illness

So I find it to be a law that when I want to do what is good, evil lies close at hand. For I delight in the law of God in my inmost self, but I see in my members another law at war with the law of my mind, making me captive to the law of sin that dwells in my members. Wretched man that I am! Who will rescue me from this body of death? Thanks be to God through Jesus Christ our Lord! So then, with my mind I am a slave to the law of God, but with my flesh I am a slave to the law of sin.

Romans 7.21–25

We have already noted that, in comparison to previous eras, we pay scant regard to sin, although we still decry its results.

Sin loomed large for Julian –
sin and the devil:
shut up in her cell
in medieval Norwich,
so far removed from us –
in time, in place,
in lifestyle, in mindset.
Today we diminish them both,
their presence, their power,
even their existence.

Today we don't prostrate ourselves
before anyone, not even God,
as a wretched sinner.

Today we stand up for our rights;
we are people of worth;
the world owes us . . .
And today we suffer still,
from loneliness, stress, depression
and meaninglessness.

Based on Chapter 82

We might have downgraded sin, but we still live with its effects.
And those of us who are trying to live our lives more fully in Christ
are well aware of our own sin. It is like a chronic illness that makes
itself felt every day, in varying degrees; it won't go away; we have to
learn to live with it by managing it in order to diminish its effects.
But in spite of this chronic disease of the soul, this is precisely where
our Lord chooses to dwell. Julian calls it the city where he has his
throne, like the medieval bishop who had his cathedral and throne
in the city.

Her conclusion from this is not to belittle our sin but not to get
hung up on it either.

And therefore he wants us promptly to attend to the touching
of his grace, rejoicing more in his unbroken love than sorrowing over our frequent failings.

For it is the greatest glory to him of anything which we
can do that we live gladly and happily for love of him in our
penance.

Colledge & Walsh, Chapter 81, page 337

We know that, while we are here on this earth,
even though we have committed ourselves to Christ,
even though we have received forgiveness
and the gift of the Spirit,

we are still sinful human beings.
We strive for transformation, for perfection,
but again and again we fail.

Yet despite all of this,
Christ looks upon us with such tender love
that he accepts all our life here as penance –
in fact, he produces this penance in us
and helps us to bear it.
He wants us to move beyond
the pain we feel each time we fail,
and fix our hearts in trust
on the joy he gives.

Based on Chapter 81

Our life is penance, declares Julian, as we live with the chronic condition of sin, and try to control it. How do we do this? How do we manage a chronic illness? By disciplining ourselves to take our medicine every day. What is the medicine that Julian recommends?

He loves us continually and we sin habitually, and he shows this to us most gently, and then we quietly sorrow and groan, turning to contemplate his mercy, hanging on to his love and his goodness, realizing that this is our medicine, while all that we do is sin.

Chapter 82

Julian can speak to us today,
from her cell in medieval Norwich.
She can speak to us Christians,
to us who want to love Christ wholly,
but keep on failing.

We know deep down that we are sinners
and always will be.
Let us acknowledge this.

Julian was shown that
Christ looks on us with pity, not with blame,
for in this passing life he does not demand
that we live life wholly without sin.
Despite our inadequacy
he loves us deeply and endlessly,
and gently shows us where we fail,
and how we can recognize his mercy,
and hang on to his love and goodness.
For though the sickness of our sin is chronic,
this is our medicine –
this is the way to fulfilment and joy.

Based on Chapter 82

A Prayer

Is this picture of sin being a 'chronic disease' helpful to you at all? What do you feel you need the most to manage the problems you face in your day-to-day life? Bring them to Christ and 'hang on to his love and goodness' while you are open to his lead in helping you to find the way through.

Meditation 39

Our Faith is a Light

This is the message we have heard from him and proclaim to you, that God is light and in him there is no darkness at all. If we say that we have fellowship with him while we are walking in darkness, we lie and do not do what is true; but if we walk in the light as he himself is in the light, we have fellowship with one another, and the blood of Jesus his Son cleanses us from all sin.

1 John 1.5–7

Now faith is the assurance of things hoped for, the conviction of things not seen.

Hebrews 11.1

From the picture of living with a chronic illness, Julian now turns to another as she brings together all she has learnt from her showings. We walk in darkness in this life and we long for more light. She talks about this earlier when in the vision of Christ on the cross she strains to see his bloodstained face. She wants more light of day to see more clearly, and is answered that God would be her light when he wanted to show her more (Chapter 10).

Don't we all long for more light? To see into the future; to see the path ahead; to see the dangers that lurk in dark places so that we can avoid them; to see what effect we have on others? To Julian we do have a light – it is faith. Maybe as you come to this point in your journey with Julian, you may feel that your faith is now brighter, and you are better able to accept the fact that your walk will be mostly in the dark.

If our life in this world,
where sin and evil predominate,
is like living in the night,
our faith is a light
in which our Mother Jesus,
the source of all light,
and the Holy Spirit, lead us.
They do not dazzle us completely,
but shed on us as much light as we need
in order to do our work.

The night is the cause of our pain and woe;
the light is the cause of our life.
Our faith enables us to walk and work in this light
with strength and wisdom:
this light which is God,
Our Endless Day.

Based on Chapters 83, 84

Even though our faith is a light and we are led by the Father, Son and Holy Spirit, there are so many mysteries that still remain unsolved. Do you have, as I have, a whole list of questions you are going to ask our Lord one day when we see him in Heaven? Julian certainly was full of questions, and God assured her that the time will come when all mysteries will be revealed.

We know that God's ways are not our ways:
that we move in this dark world of ours
with our eyes blinded by sin and

misted over with the tears of our sorrows,
stumbling along,
bewildered and unsure,
full of questions, murmuring,
'If only it would have been like this and not that,
then all would have been well',
as we try to follow the path we dimly see,
illuminated by what little faith we have
and God's grace.

For faith enables us to believe,
despite all else,
that God created us in love,
and in that same love protects us,
and never allows us to be hurt
to the extent that all our
joy is extinguished.

Faith enables us to believe
that one day we shall clearly see
in God the mysteries that are
now hidden from us,
and the answers to all our questions.

Then we shall say,
'Lord, blessed may you be,
because it was as it was, it is well,
in all manner of things it is well.'
Then we shall see that
from without beginning it was all held
in our Lord's loving hands.

Based on Chapter 85

Till then we live by faith, with all our unanswered questions, with all our unsolved mysteries. Our God is light but our faith is the switch that turns on the light of God in our lives.

A Prayer

Lord, I think of those times when you have led me through green pastures and still waters, the sun shedding its warmth and its light to revive my spirit. My faith has been strong and joyous. Thank you for those times.

But Lord, I also think of those times when I have walked through a valley dark as death and stumbled along, blinded by tears, longing for an arm to lean on and more light, my faith like a torch with nearly dead batteries.

Come, God, my Father, my endless day, shed light on my way.

Come, Jesus, my Mother, take my hand and lead me.

Come Holy Spirit, fill me and strengthen me, open my eyes and make my way clear.

And today, whatever the day brings, recharge the light of my faith. Amen.

Meditation 40

Love Was His Meaning

If I speak in the tongues of mortals and of angels, but do not have love, I am a noisy gong or a clanging cymbal. And if I have prophetic powers, and understand all mysteries and all knowledge, and if I have all faith, so as to remove mountains, but do not have love, I am nothing. If I give away all my possessions, and if I hand over my body so that I may boast, but do not have love, I gain nothing . . . Love never ends. But as for prophecies, they will come to an end; as for tongues, they will cease; as for knowledge, it will come to an end . . . And now faith, hope, and love abide, these three; and the greatest of these is love.

1 Corinthians 13.1–3, 8, 13

Julian has told us – as she has told her fellow Christians, those who will be saved, and especially those who are called to a life of contemplation – what she herself was shown by God regarding human nature: how we are nobly and honourably made, how God dwells in us and we in God, yet how we will never be rid of sin in this life, but always yearn to be more united with God. She has told us what she was shown regarding God's nature; he is triune; he is our Lord and we are his servants; he is our Father and Mother who never stops loving us and looks at us with pity and not blame.

She sees that the contemplation of our Lord God will enable us to accept our limitations as we live for him each day, and maybe we have come to see this in our lives as well. She is given one final insight:

We cannot know God
unless he shows himself to us –
so that in some way we see him;
unless he touches us –
so that in some way we understand him;
unless he calls us –
so that in some way we feel his presence.

Our God shows that
he is life, in wonderful familiarity,
that he is love, in ever gentle concern for us,
that he is light, in his unending kindness.

All three aspects are united in one goodness.
Oh, how we long to be part of that unity,
and with such longing we cling to him
with all our strength.

Based on Chapter 83

It is God who initiated the showings, and having received them and thought deeply about them, Julian kept on asking what her Lord meant by giving them to her. This was her quest for fifteen years she tells us, and then she received an answer:

In Julian's illness,
in her showings,
in her life of solitude,

as year followed year,
she wrestled with the question,
'What does it all mean?'
'What is our Lord's meaning in all this?'

In our life,
in its ups and downs,
in the flashes of insight we are given,
the depths of sorrow into which we sink,
we also want to know,
'What does it all mean?'

The answer came to Julian
in her spiritual understanding,
'Love was his meaning.
Know it well.
Who showed all this to you?
It was Love.
What did he show you?
It was Love.
Why did he show it to you?
For Love.'

So Julian saw very certainly,
in this and in everything,
that before God made us he loved us,
and he goes on loving us
with a love that never lets go
and never will.

May we, each one,
see for ourselves, as certainly,
that the meaning of all is Love:

that we are all held in God's love,
with a love that never lets go,
and never will.

Based on Chapter 86

So Julian sums up all her showings in the one word – love. She sees, though, that this love is given to her, not so that she can sit back and bask in it:

For I saw and understood clearly that our Lord meant to have all that he showed better known than it is. In this knowledge he wants to give us grace to love him and to cleave to him.

Chapter 86

Julian did just that by writing down her experiences and insights. And she concludes that this book was begun by a gift of God and in his grace, but it is not yet fully worked out.

For the sake of love, let us all join with God's working in prayer, thanking, trusting and rejoicing, for so our good Lord would have us pray.

Chapter 86

May you continue your journey with Julian of Norwich as a friend, enriched by any new ways in which she has helped you to see yourself, your faith, your fellow Christians and your Lord.

A Prayer

Lord, I thank you for all your showings of love to this dear lady, Julian, and how I have come to know about it myself. I thank you for the many gifts and graces you have given me.

I pause to thank you for some in particular.

I trust in your unending love, as my Father, as my Mother, as my familiar friend, as my light to guide me and protect me. Continue to watch over me and to help me to grow into closer unity with you. I pause to ask for some things in particular.

I rejoice in your love, your presence, your gifts, your constancy, your beauty. Even in the worst of times, help me never to lose the ability to rejoice. I pause to think of some things in particular.

Help me to make the whole meaning of my life one of love. Amen.

Bibliography

Edmund Colledge OSA and James Walsh SJ (trans.), 1978, *Julian of Norwich: Showings*, translated from the critical text with an introduction, in The Classics of Western Spirituality series, Paulist Press, 1978, The missionary Society of St Paul the Apostle in the State of New York. (referred to in the text as Colledge & Walsh).

Father John-Julian OJN (Order of Julian of Norwich), 1988, *A Lesson of Love: The Revelations of Julian of Norwich, edited and translated for devotional use*, Darton, Longman & Todd.

Father John-Julian OJN, 2009, *The Complete Julian of Norwich*, Paraclete Press. This is the most comprehensive attempt to offer a modern translation of Julian's writings as well as a substantial body of research into the historical, religious and personal background material that illuminates her life and work.

Grace M. Jantzen, 1987, *Julian of Norwich: Mystic and Theologian*, SPCK.

Index of Bible Readings

Index of First Lines of Poems

Index of Chapters from *Showings*

Index of Chapters from Showings